HUMANITY
IN
GOD

HUMANITY
IN
GOD

Elisabeth Moltmann-Wendel
Jürgen Moltmann

SCM PRESS LTD

*Scripture quotations are from the
Revised Standard Version of the Bible,
copyright 1946, 1952 and © 1971
by the Division of Christian Education, National Council of Churches,
and are used by permission.*

334 02055 7

Originally delivered as the E. T. Earl Lectures
at the Pacific School of Religion, Berkeley, California
First published in Great Britain 1984
by SCM Press Ltd
26–30 Tottenham Road London N1

Typeset in The United States of America
and printed in Great Britain by
The Camelot Press Ltd
Southampton

CONTENTS

ILLUSTRATIONS

FOREWORD

Elisabeth Moltmann-Wendel and Jürgen Moltmann have been published separately many times. This is the first occasion, however, when readers can find them in the same volume and encounter them in dialogue about theological concerns they share. We are delighted to have had a part in arranging for them to deliver the Earl Lectures in Berkeley and now to contribute an introduction to this culmination of their joint endeavor.

The work of Jürgen Moltmann, since 1967 professor of systematic theology in the University of Tübingen, Germany, became widely known in the United States following his emergence as a major theological figure in the midsixties with the publication of his *Theology of Hope*. He has steadily increased in stature through his continuing contributions to Christian doctrine, political theology, and social ethics. Many now regard him as the most influential living Protestant theologian, not only in Europe and North America, but also—indeed especially—in Latin America, Asia, and Africa.

Elisabeth Moltmann-Wendel—teacher, speaker, and free-lance

writer—is among the small but growing number of women who have gained entrance into the male-dominated world of theology. Her prophetic voice is well known in the churches of Germany as a leader in Christian thought and life. Increasingly over the past decade, she has been raising issues related to the women's movement in the church and, since the publication of her *Liberty, Equality, Sisterhood: On the Emancipation of Women in Church and Society*, is becoming widely known as an incisive feminist theologian. She has translated and edited for German readers theological writings from the American women's movement, and her influence in this country is increasing.

Publication side by side in this book of the work of these two distinguished theologians is part of a journey together they began when they met as theological students at the University of Göttingen in 1948. Jürgen, born in Hamburg, April 8, 1926, had arrived there by way of a boyhood spent in northern Germany and shattering teenage experiences in World War II and as a prisoner of war in Britain. Elisabeth Wendel was born in Potsdam (now part of East Germany) on July 25, 1926. The granddaughter of a Prussian pastor, she lived with her family in the vicinity of Berlin throughout her early life, including the harsh war years. When the war ended she began her study of theology, first at Berlin and then at Göttingen. After their marriage Jürgen and Elisabeth continued their studies, and both received doctorates in theology from Göttingen in the early 1950s.

Jürgen served first as pastor of a Reformed Church in Bremen and then as a professor on theological faculties in Wuppertal and Bonn before moving to Tübingen in 1967. During these years Elisabeth pursued her career as a free-lance writer and speaker, while giving primary attention to their home and a growing family of four daughters. By 1970, when Jürgen was developing and extending motifs from his theology of hope into new areas, including the ecumenical context, Elisabeth was relating issues of hope to the feminist movement. Her interest developed as she responded to needs of women in her own church in southern Germany—speaking, writing, participating in consultations, trying to give them a sense of themselves as members of the Body of Christ with the right and responsibility to speak out. From there she made connection with the wider women's movement, where she has continued to work.

The title for this book, *Humanity in God*, reflects the orientation of both Jürgen Moltmann and Elisabeth Moltmann-Wendel. They bring to their work not only strong grounding in Bible, theology, and history, but also the experiences of their own lives and their shared passion for freedom from oppression. Each of them develops this theme in a quite different way, suggesting their own distinctive styles.

Elisabeth Moltmann-Wendel's series is called "Women Experiencing God." Here she builds on and extends her earlier work researching female figures in the New Testament, especially Mary Magdalene and Martha, published as *Women Around Jesus*. As she traces the distorted interpretations of these women and the surprising roles they play in the Middle Ages, she calls attention to the dominant patriarchal structure of the Christian church but makes vivid the matriarchal substructure that has remained throughout our history and has preserved a vision that can renew our faith today. Because she is working with the intangible, underside of our past she is charting a new course for doing theology by appealing to artistic feeling and interpretation, looking not only at what the Bible says, but also at what has not been written there, listening to experiences of women and other victims of male oppression. Jesus' message has revolutionary potential for women, she points out, and when we strip away the patriarchal distortions of tradition, we will find in him the model for male-female relationships. Without the free and equal participation of women in all areas of life there can be no wholeness to our humanity.

Jürgen Moltmann, in his series entitled "God with the Human Face," continues the fascinating combination of biblical, historical, and theological ethical scholarship with sensitive concern for the oppressed that gives him his distinctive power as a global Christian thinker. Even as he throws new and imaginative light on biblical texts and historical issues, he maintains a vivid awareness of the significance for Christian faith of the cries from the depths of human misery and of Jesus' abandonment on the cross. Extending especially the thought of *The Crucified God* and *The Trinity and the Kingdom*, he shows that biblical faith means liberation and only through faith in the God of the crucified and risen Jesus Christ can we distinguish the true meaning of freedom; that the notion of the triune God is not only present in the New Testament story of Jesus, rather than added later, but also provides the basis for overcoming patriarchalism in the church and for understanding the nature of human community; and that the social understanding of the Trinity can lead to the recovery of wholeness in our view of humans and of society. Nowhere in his work to date do we find the close relation among biblical faith, theological reflection, and human liberation more brilliantly expressed.

In the Moltmanns' dialogue, "Becoming Human in New Community," we have a miniblueprint for the kind of work the church must do if it is to become a viable expression of our humanity in God. Elisabeth's remarks are often personal, dramatic, and critical; Jürgen's responses usually evoke a sense of reasonable, historical perspective. Where he might tend to blur the problem of women's oppression by leaping too quickly to the need for joint liberation, she presses the point that women have been the ones who lacked power and self-identity. When she despairs over the ability of the church to change its patriarchal structure, he emphasizes sources that support feminine presence in deity and the fact that Christianity lives from hope as well as tradition. Jürgen sees that men must let go both their masculine privileges and their sense of male-oriented responsibilities; Elisabeth knows that women must learn to trust themselves and their own experiences. And both of them affirm that it is by being faithful to Jesus that the Spirit enables us to change and brings us into liberating community.

When the Moltmanns spoke to the thousand or more people attending Pacific School of Religion's Earl Lectures and Pastoral Conference, the atmosphere crackled with excitement. There were gales of laughter, groans of recognition, and frequent bursts of applause throughout Elisabeth's series as she showed us our own image in the distorted mirror of patriarchal interpretation. For Jürgen, the response was more subdued and quiet, while we followed the step-by-step progression of his thought as he reinterpreted traditional beliefs in new theological perspective. But in their joint lecture we all watched and listened as though present at a good jam session. The themes were introduced, developed, and reworked antiphonally, as first one and then the other took the lead and set the tone. The meaning of their dialogue, however, was not so much in whether they resolved the discords between men and women, oppression and liberation, church structures and life experience. What gave us hope was the music of their modeling as they spoke to each other with trust, respect, and honesty. Their styles were different—as all of ours are—but their commitment to becoming human in a new community as man and woman in equal partnership was the same— as all of ours can be.

Charles S. McCoy and Marjorie Casebier McCoy
Berkeley, California

Charles S. McCoy is Robert Gordon Sproul Professor of Theological Ethics at Pacific School of Religion and director of the Center for Ethics and Social Policy at the Graduate Theological Union. Marjorie Casebier McCoy is a free-lance author, actress, and teacher and is currently an adjunct faculty member at Pacific School of Religion.

PREFACE

In February 1982, at the invitation of the Pacific School of Religion, Berkeley, California, we presented the following lectures as the E.T. Earl Lectures in conjunction with a pastors' conference. Since that time, some of the lectures have been given individually as the Beth Anne Harnish Memorial Lectures in Fresno and as the Gordon E. Michalson Lectures at the Claremont School of Theology. Publication in this form is an expression of our appreciation for these generous invitations.

When we accepted the invitation to join in giving the Earl Lectures, we were aware that we were setting out on a new adventure. We could not then be sure of the outcome, which we are now publishing in this book. Here, for the first time, we are trying to bring our diverse theological paths into convergence and to articulate the common ground of our living and thinking. It had never been our intent to express what we hold in common by using the same language and identical concepts or symbols. On the contrary, we did not want to ignore or suppress divergences and differences.

Each of us was to speak for herself and himself, but we wanted to do so together. The last, joint lecture is an attempt in this direction. By being open to each other and to an ongoing journey of discovering what belongs to each of us and what we hold in common, we hope to encourage our hearers and readers to venture out for themselves, to begin their own dialogue with one another, so that "sons and daughters shall prophesy," as the prophet Joel has promised, and that women and men shall see visions of a new, more humane future.

Elisabeth and Jürgen Moltmann
Tübingen

Elisabeth Moltmann-Wendel

WOMEN EXPERIENCING GOD

1

Mary Magdalene—
An Example of
Patriarchal Distortion
of History

The feminist theological research emerging from "women's studies" has brought to light two basic facts: (1) Many early churches were communities of women and men in which the women were equal to the men and had tasks as apostles, bishops, and leaders of congregations.[1] (2) Christian theology, as transmitted to us, has certain dominating patriarchal features, and the church is permeated with patriarchal habits of thought, relationship patterns, and life-styles. I call patriarchal cultures where the males and the allegedly masculine traits of rationality and willpower have priority over nature and over the females and allegedly feminine traits.

Since research has shown that the initial Jesus movement was a nonascetic, charismatic phenomenon in which women and men followed the itinerant preacher Jesus, who addressed the most varied fringe groups and, above all, entered into real partnerships with women, there has been increased interest in when and where patriarchalization of the movement and its documents set in. In many parts of the New Testament there are sexist statements about women that, for example, subordinate them to men and even defame them.

The question of when and where patriarchalization enters is a question for historical research, but for many women today it is important to discover whether the church as an institution, under which so many have suffered, was initially different in its basic structure and whether the gospel offers them the possibility of a fulfilling life. At the same time, the continued existence of the church is questioned, for women are asking whether the church is facing and will embrace the challenges of the social, ecological, and economic demands of feminism or whether it will remain in the ghetto of its patriarchal traditions.

New Testament research shows how Jesus' invitation to freedom was changed into a concern for order and how in the editing of the New Testament writings, traditions that were originally women's traditions were repressed.[2] Following this patriarchal editing of the New Testament, however, the gospel experienced a further patriarchalization in that it was received into a patriarchal church. Once again the Bible was integrated into the heads, hearts, and hands of a ruling class and was changed.

I wish to begin with this later patriarchalization of the Jesus tradition in order to show from the history of piety and everyday religion that the process of patriarchalization continued to develop unresisted, but that this process can be interrupted and changed. This I want to show by reference to two female figures of the New Testament. One, discussed in this chapter, is Mary Magdalene, who is known as the great sinner. The other, discussed in the next chapter, is Martha, known as the dutiful housewife. These two women are lively, colorful, and richly illustrative examples of how people today, with their present culture and self-understanding, are to deal with the gospel call to freedom and how they must measure their own traditions critically by reference to this call to freedom. Patriarchalization of the gospel still takes place, now, daily, in new ways, for example, in our sermons, in our Bible translations, and in the selection of Bible texts. Critical questioning of the past is therefore, at the same time, a critical questioning of our contemporary relationship to the content of the Bible and of our own concepts and ideas, with which we either liberate others or oppress them.

First, I want to establish what the New Testament says about

Mary Magdalene. Next, I will explore how she has been dealt with by the Christian tradition.[3]

THE BIBLICAL MARY MAGDALENE

Mary Magdalene took her second name from her hometown, Magdala, a busy commercial town on the sea of Gennesaret. She suffered from a severe mental illness (see Luke 8:2), presumably epilepsy, and she was one of a group of women who began following Jesus because he had healed them. Her healing had been salvation for her. It was different for the men who were called to leave their jobs to begin an itinerant existence as Jesus' disciples. (There are no reports of a male disciple who was healed and thus called.) Like the other healed women who followed Jesus, Mary Magdalene served Jesus just as Jesus came to serve and to give his life. Her whole being is imbued with discipleship. But it is never said of the male disciples that they "serve" Jesus as Jesus "had served" them.

When any of the four Gospel writers refers to the group of women around Jesus, Mary Magdalene's name is always listed first. She had characteristics of leadership, and Luke records that she brought financial resources with her. The Jewish women, no longer protected by a family headed by a male, turned to her for guidance. From the later Gospels one senses Mary Magdalene's growing authority, which made the disciples—Peter above all—furious. The Gospels, which normally emphasize different heroines, all report that Mary Magdalene stood with the women at the cross, was there when Jesus was buried, and was first at the tomb on Easter morning. All this indicates her special relation to Jesus. Among the women, she has been accorded a more favored position: The resurrected Jesus shows himself to her and commissions her to tell the other diciples that he is raised. Matthew (28:1) adds "the other Mary," and Luke (24:10) says that other women disciples, including Joanna, were present. But the writers of Mark (16) and of John (20) report the special Jesus-Mary Magdalene encounters that provide the basis of her unique place in Christian history.

I want to investigate three elements of the story of Mary Magdalene in the tradition: her commission to proclaim, her healing and

5

calling, and her exceptional relationship with Jesus. What has Christianity made of all that? How did it come about that Mary Magdalene became the exemplary "great sinner"?

THE PREACHING MARY MAGDALENE

New Testament research has proven that there were women apostles in the early church, for example, Junias (Romans 16)[4] and Martha (John 11).[5] Testimony by witnesses both early and late indicates that Mary Magdalene, who played an important role among Jesus' followers, became one of the primary examples of this apostleship. As the Vatican today is agitated by such issues, so too Peter, as predecessor of the popes, became insecure and angry that a woman should usurp what he regarded as a masculine position.

This conflict over the place of privilege and the man-woman conflict are dealt with more openly in later Gospels not included in the New Testament canon. Peter stands out as an angry, envious, bad-tempered opponent. In the "Pistis Sophia"[6] he complains to Jesus: "My Lord, we can no longer stand this woman. She takes away from us every opportunity to speak. She talks constantly." Or, "Did he [the Savior] really speak privately with a woman and not openly to us? Are we to turn around and all listen to her?" he grumbles in the "Gospel According to Mary Magdalene."[7] As Mary Magdalene breaks down and weeps, protesting that she did not dream up her encounter with Jesus, another disciple acts as mediator in the conflict. He says that Peter should not treat the woman like an adversary, that certainly Jesus knows her completely and has placed her not only above all women, but also above his friends.

In the experience of the early church, as reported in apocryphal writings, Mary Magdalene appears to surpass the men. Acts of the Apostles describes an angel encouraging the disciples, while the apocryphal material depicts Mary Magdalene as inspiring the powerless disciples, who do not know how to begin to fulfill the commission to preach.[8] But things changed. The early churches took on the patriarchal structures of their surroundings, and the early role of women was forgotten.

During the Middle Ages, however, the masculine preaching tradition, which had come to be accepted as a matter of course, was interrupted for a short time. In southern France there grew up legends about Mary Magdalene in which her role as the missionary saint of France stood out ever more clearly.[9] According to the earliest legends of the eleventh century, Mary Magdalene, having been driven out of Palestine, went with her spiritual head, Maximin, into the French region of Provence. Initially, Maximin is actually the head pastor, who both baptizes and preaches, but Mary emancipates herself from her clerical lord and, in the second series of the legend, begins to preach, convert, and baptize. She takes an active missionary role, converting the princely rulers of Marseilles and their pagan subjects and thereby becomes the central character of the legend cycle in southern France. Her actual apostolic function—proclamation of the resurrection to the disciples—is revived in these legends.

Stained-glass windows of thirteenth-century French cathedrals portray this rediscovery of Mary Magdalene.[10] The legendary story of the saint is presented in cycles, out of which—despite infiltration by foreign medieval features—the characteristics of the New Testament image constantly appear. In the Cathedral of Chartres, Mary Magdalene appears (ca. 1230) as a saint with a halo, while the sermon is preached by Maximin. In Auxerre, thirty years later, Mary Magdalene preaches as Maximin stands nearby. Her clerical companion has been relegated to a less prominent place, but the role of the male hierarchy is protected, for Maximin still baptizes. By the end of the thirteenth century Mary Magdalene is presented with Martha—both as preachers—in the windows of the cathedral of Semur in Burgundy. Finally, at Châlons-sur-Marne, in the sixteenth century, a picture appears in which she baptizes. Her lost role has been returned to her.

Pictures of a preaching Mary Magdalene are to be encountered in Florence, Graubünden, Lübeck, and Donaueschingen. The Lübeck depiction includes a further clerical duty; there she consecrates her brother Lazarus as the Bishop of Marseilles.

Mary Magdalene regained her commission to proclaim the resurrection, but not for long. With the Reformation this short but impressive emancipation came to an end.

How did it happen that art could disregard the prohibition forbidding women to speak in the congregation? The answer is that the pictures of Mary Magdalene as preacher and with priestly func-

7

The Preaching Mary Magdalene in France

Mary Magdalene Consecrating Lazarus a Bishop of Marseilles

tions are images that accompanied the medieval women's movement which developed new life-styles over against the male hierarchy of the church. In groups like the Cathari and the Waldenses, who rebelled against the hierarchical church, women founded new communities.[11] Here one encounters women who preach and who discuss theology openly, and thus reflect the missionary Mary Magdalene.

Do the Mary Magdalene legends and the corresponding art come out of such communities? In any case, there is here—as in some early Christian Gnostic circles—a lower estimation of Mary the mother of Jesus, with unconventional saints taking her place.

Even during the Inquisition, when many sect members—especially women—suffered persecution, the tenacity of Mary Magdalene is often noted. It is striking that the Magdalene cult and the Cathari and the Waldensian women's movements arose at the same time and that they drew on the same image, a changed image, of women. This new image was the responsibility-bearing, preaching woman that had been rejected by the church as a possibility for women. Mary Magdalene won the hearts and heads of those in these medieval feminist groups, and her charismatic personality, forgotten for centuries, like Sleeping Beauty, was awakened.

Setbacks for women occurred in these sects, however, during the thirteenth century, as hierarchical development took place. Added to this was the bloody persecution of the Cathari, which brought a premature end to the whole movement that had been supportive of women. In the art of the periods following this development, the independent spiritual image of woman represented by Mary Magdalene appeared occasionally, but her rights were now curtailed. A male cleric once again took over as director of the convent, and public preaching was submerged until the twentieth century. Only documents of the early church and isolated pictures of medieval art have maintained Mary Magdalene's commission to proclaim the resurrection.

SEXUAL SYMBOLISM IN MARY MAGDALENE'S ILLNESS AND HEALING

The church has dealt even less adequately with the demonic sickness of a woman who was close to Jesus. Demonic possession in a woman

10

could be interpreted as nothing else than unbridled passion—lust, carnality, licentious sexuality. Mary Magdalene's illness (Luke 8:2) was identified as a form of sexual obsession. She was merged with the woman sinner (Luke 7:37) and with the anointing Mary of Bethany (John 12:3).

As a result, the greatest and—for women—the most effective patriarchal distortion of history in western Europe was complete. Mary Magdalene had been made into the exemplary monster and model of sin and sexuality because her dazzling, privileged, and unique story offered the possibility of releasing imaginative fantasies.

The equating of the three biblical women was, however, unknown to the fathers of the early church (e.g., Irenaeus, Origen, Chrysostom). They praised Mary Magdalene as "Apostle of all Apostles." According to Karl Künstle, the confusing of the three women goes back to Augustine, "who gladly did this to them for psychological reasons, because it must have been a consolation to him that the Lord stayed so often with Mary at Bethany, even though she—like him [Augustine]—once lay in the bonds of sensuality."[12]

Male fantasy and male conflicts shaped Christian tradition and theology. It appears that Bishop Ambrose and others of his time, representing a moralistic trend in the church, were responsible for the development of a new interpretation of the relation between body and spirit. Pope Gregory's Magdalene homilies of A.D. 600 completed this process by combining in a single image "the remorseful sinner, the ardent Mary of Bethany and the loving Mary Magdalene."[13] Thenceforth, with papal authority, an idealized concept of woman is set forth in which Mary Magdalene becomes the "most striking illustration revealing the help of divine grace that leads to penance and hope."[14] The "great sinner" (*magna peccatrix*) Mary Magdalene appears; she personifies the sin of the world and wears a headband that declares, "Don't despair because you have sinned. By my example renew yourself for God."

We see this now as the violation of an integrated image of woman. (How would men feel today if Peter were interpreted as a gigolo?) The artificial image of Mary was intended to reveal moral needs, but her story could no longer be read without serious distortion. Wasn't Peter with his betrayal a more vivid example of sin and forgiveness? Or the corrupt tax collector Zacchaeus? Would not the

11

abandonment of friends or the cruelty of social injustice provide a better illustration of sinful human nature?

Western European theology erroneously and unambiguously placed sin in the human body, especially in the body of woman. The outcome of this mistake has contributed to the notion of woman's inferiority. Women in western European culture tend to be self-deprecating, even in the present. Greek theologians, by contrast, consistently maintained the distinction among the three women and as a result have retained many multisided, colorful images of woman. Equating the "noble woman, Mary of Bethany" with a prostitute contradicted both their appreciation and their regard for women.

The Roman Breviary cultivated the western European image until recently, when the misrepresentation of the biblical picture was acknowledged. But the European history of morals and manners—the social history, the history of art and literature—is shaped by that image. Magdalene cloisters, sanctuaries, and homes for "fallen women" evidence this tradition. Mary Magdalene became the literary and pictorial symbol for immorality.

The attempt to separate these three women figures again, which has been going on since the end of the Middle Ages, most often has failed. Rather than following the lead of the enlightened Faber Stapulensis, Martin Luther chose to use the distorted image of Mary Magdalene held by the church to illustrate his doctrines of sin and grace. Protestant theologians, more critically aware of the Bible, saw the fallacy of the popular tradition more readily than their Roman Catholic counterparts. Still, contemporary opinion shows that a long tradition of biblical criticism has done little to combine the name of Mary Magdalene with anything other than the title "the great sinner."

Alongside the notion of the great sinner, the image of the penitent arose quickly. Mary Magdalene is shown wearing a hair shirt as penance for her sin, from which she experiences divine grace. With this portrayal a further fateful development was introduced. Mary Magdalene's penitence became the exemplary image for the way a Christian is to relate body and soul. Material, bodily existence is condemned, and the transcendental is glorified; the subjugation of the earth and the triumph of the soul over the earthly is celebrated. In this picture of her "the early Christian sought . . . to free the soul from its bondage to the body, in order to make its climb into the pure spiritual kingdom of the divine easier."[15] For example, those joining the Crusades could visit a center for pilgrims in southern France consecrated to her and receive a special blessing from her picture. At this place Bernard of Clairvaux preached the triumph of the Christian cross over paganism. Mary Magdalene was the symbol of the spirit's triumph over the world used by both Cluny and the Franciscans to reform the church.

From among the various presentations of Mary Magdalene, the picture that became sanctioned by the church was her elevation: She floats above the earth, with cherubs supporting and lifting her; the sinner has overcome the world. This picture is often wrongly explained as Mary Magdalene's ascension, whereas it actually depicts her heavenly elevation in prayer, a scene from the legend cycle of southern France mentioned previously. The acceptance of this spiritualized Mary Magdalene, which took place between the late Middle Ages and the baroque period—and popularized during the Reformation, when copies of Albrecht Dürer's woodcut of the "elevation" were sold at the markets—brought to an end the controversial story of Mary Magdalene. "She was surrendered to the transcendental world," says a modern Catholic guide to saints. The flight from the dangerous world of senses and sensuality into heavenly purity was successful, but at the cost of repressing the body. Mary Magdalene could encounter us as a completely healed human person, but we are still suffering under a theology that separates body and spirit and is incapable of discovering humanity in its completeness and wholeness as God's good creation.

THE LOVER OF JESUS

For a long time the Easter morning meeting between Jesus and Mary Magdalene recounted in the Gospel of John has encouraged speculation about a possible intimacy between them. In their short exchange his "Mary" and her "Teacher" suggest a rapture, joy, and eroticism that exceed the teacher-disciple relationship.

Mary Magdalene has filled a fundamental desire for an erotic dimension not overtly present in the New Testament. She had to play the role of Aphrodite in Christianity, and in a Christianity made anxious by sexuality, she still satisfies these erotic needs. Perhaps herein lies her clearest, most natural and human role. In this role Mary Magdalene was the patroness of the medieval cosmetic industry. Perfume-makers, ointment-producers, and hairdressers placed themselves under her care. She protected the production of fashionable accessories, such as purses, combs, and gloves, essential to the fascinating charm of females. Artists painted her in elegant, flowing dresses decorated with jewelry. In some pictures of the sixteenth and seventeenth centuries she stands half-nude in front of a mirror, admiring her own beauty. Along with the judgment that this is empty vanity, one senses, even in a prudish Christianity, the pleasure and zest that depict the fun side of life. The beautiful Helen of Christianity skips along at the side of her lover; she rides in the hunt and becomes, when emancipated from the church, a picture of purest delight to the senses.

In recent years the question of whether Jesus had an intimate relationship with Mary Magdalene has been fervently discussed. The imaginative speculation that John evoked was, however, spiritually sublimated: Mary Magdalene, bride of Christ, was engaged but never married; for the spiritualized bride and bridegroom it was a promised but unconsummated marriage. Luther found this to say about her earthly love for Jesus: "She can think, dream, talk of nothing else but him; if I only had the man as my most beloved guest and lord, my heart would be content."[16] She "loved him with a hearty, lusting, rutting love"; she had a "hot, lusting, rutting heart for him." These expressions allow us to suppose that Luther assumed sexual intercourse between them. When he expounds on their "daily companionship," however, their intimacy is not earthly but spiritual.[17] The world *familiaritas*, which Luther uses here, he finally translates as "brotherhood," which seems to indicate that he imagined a spiritual friendship between the two. This may not have excluded sexual intercourse, for she had "goodness and honor, body and life—everything—staked on him." But above all else, Luther wanted to show her total, spontaneous, passionate self-giving to Jesus.

After the Enlightenment, Mary Magdalene as the "great lover" came to be taken more and more for granted. There was less emphasis on her relationship with Jesus. In France, particularly, her story was that of the courtesan who loved much and thus gave much away. In German literature of the last century, through the work of Nobel Prize winner Paul von Heyse, she became an Epicurean who saw her fulfillment in sensuality.

Because of the need to recover the sensual and the erotic in Christianity, theologians have begun to see Mary Magdalene as a lover. That which no other image of woman achieves and which Mary's motherly love does not uncover breaks out again with Heinrich Böll's emphasis on Mary Magdalene's tenderness. A Christianity that is positively supportive of sexuality, that attends to human beings and their needs, must check its moral laws again. Justice will not be done to Mary Magdalene if she is pinned down to great love and sacrifice. If she is typed with "tenderness," she will simply be misused as a compensation by a rough, cruel world.

If she were used merely to satisfy erotic needs, she would become monodimensional. Mary Magdalene as a tender plus to a cruel story of crucifixion and a patriarchal world completely misses the total view of the New Testament and avoids its women. Mary Magdalene and the women appear as helpless therapists in the rock opera *Jesus Christ Superstar*, offering the agonized, desolate Jesus what no man can provide. "She alone has tried to give me what I need right here and now," Jesus says in the drama. "There is not a man among you who knows or cares whether I come or go." These "therapists" console Jesus. Mary Magdalene urges him not to struggle but to shut his eyes, to cease thinking, and to let the world be itself, while the other women murmur: "Everything is O.K., yes, everything is fine."

Mary Magdalene is not only a trusted female companion of Jesus. As her erotic characteristics are acknowledged they become part of her wholeness as a person. Thus the erotic elements are liberated from the confines of a constricted view of sexuality and may now permeate the different and various parts of life.

The New Testament image of Mary Magdalene which now clearly confronts us has broken conventions—for a patriarchal theology— in a dangerous way: Mary Magdalene as a woman preacher, as one healed in body, as lover of Jesus. A 2,000-year-old history of male fantasies has painted over and distorted the original story. This compares only with the process in which the matriarchal goddesses were patriarchalized and changed from universality to sexual roles.

A church that is returning to women their original commission to preach, a theology that reconciles body and spirit, an ethic that sees not only marriage, but also friendship as human community cannot avoid the image of Mary Magdalene. Her theology, however, is not yet written.

2
Martha—
A Forgotten Medieval
Tradition

A PROTESTANT WOMEN'S PROBLEM

My interest in Martha began when women's groups wanted to hear something new about biblical women, and I wanted to bring them closer to the new picture of Mary the mother of Jesus. I noticed that the women identified not with the mother of Jesus but with Martha—*Martha*, the hostess whom Jesus visited and who worked in the kitchen while her sister Mary was listening to Jesus; *Martha*, whom Jesus scolded because she wanted her sister to help her; *Martha*, the useful, active, necessary, but obviously devalued woman. For "*Mary* [not Martha] has chosen the good portion" [Luke 10:42]. Women *wanted* to be like Mary—listening, sitting, resting—but they *had to be* like Martha—acting, caring, cooking.

This negative identification caused me to follow up the biblical image of Martha. In so doing I discovered that apart from the Mary-Martha story in Luke, with its negative effects on women (Luke 10:38–42), there is also a very positive picture of Martha in the Johannine story (John 11:1–44). There Martha, strong of faith, is

17

active and guiding, the one who forced the resurrection of Lazarus to happen, a critical and passionate partner in dialogue with Jesus. As Raymond Brown has shown,[1] she makes a confession of faith in Christ which is equal to Peter's confession. I first had to discover and clarify this story with women. This story, which they knew of but didn't really know, had never been experienced by them as an *alternative* Martha story.

How has it happened that, although there are two very different stories here, only *one* type of piety and behavior has arisen? The cause may lie in our theological tradition, a tradition shaped by masculine interests. In that tradition Martha is appreciated as active and useful, but apart from that she is uninteresting and of little value. Where she speaks with greatest intensity, as in John 11, she is indeed gossipy and less sensitive than Mary.[2] The silent love of the theologians is the modestly listening Mary. Rudolf Bultmann is a positive exception in that he sees Martha as strong of faith over against Mary of little faith. "Martha's answer shows the true stance of faith."[3] Rarely is Martha's name to be found in the indexes, even when the book has come out of feminist research and when her name appears frequently in the text. Until now, theologically, she has had no worth.

In looking for pictures that depict the Martha in John 11, who is strong of faith, I stumbled on a medieval painting of Martha that had been used widely in that period: Martha the dragon conqueror.[4] This Martha no longer reminds us of the Lucan housewife who was reprimanded by Jesus. This Martha radiates peace, composure, and deliberation and looks proud, victorious, and self-aware. She is usually depicted as a fully mature woman, sometimes as a nun but also as an elegant lady of society. In Tessin there is a richly decorated baroque church with a portrayal of Martha that resembles a Greek goddess, full of the joy of life. One hand usually holds a container of holy water and a sprinkler or a cross with which she has subdued the dragon. In the other hand she holds her girdle, with which she has bound the dragon.

Martha's composure and serenity is in total contrast to the bare-toothed creature at her feet. Here the artist's imagination found a subject for the canvas full of rich possibilities. The dragon is a huge snake-monster. It looks like a primordial armor-clad beast with lion paws or webbed feet and stares cunningly up at its conqueror.

This dragon, like in a fairy tale, has wings, but they sag sorrowfully in defeat. Its fearsomeness can still be seen, however, for it is not dead, only caught, conquered, restrained, and rendered harmless. All the biblical images of animals used to symbolize evil are combined in this image: the snake, the dragon of the apocalypse, the beast from the underworld. Even in depictions of Martha where victory over the dragon is not the main motif, the dragon continues to be suggested. It has shrunk to a toy dragon in her hand on a statue in a sanctuary in Halle (East Germany). Tiny dragon imps have been painted on green clouds that form the background for Martha at the Tiefbronn Altar near Pforzheim (West Germany). These representations seem to be an interpretation and expansion of the Johannine Martha. In the medieval depictions, as in the Gospel, she has an active part in the victory over death—over the animal of the abyss. It is a picture of resurrection hope. Martha's activity is no longer defined according to her sex and thus devalued (as good housework) but is expanded to take on cosmic dimensions.

Like the Johannine Martha, this medieval picture is little known. It has been noted and treasured in France. In the German context, for instance, even though there are numerous examples in southern Germany, it is almost unknown and has had no guiding influence for women in modern times. Where it is known, it is met with a total lack of understanding: "This motif . . . opposes with very limited inspiration . . . the motif of the gentle and extraordinary figures of the Lady and the saint," states a standard work on the lives of the saints.[5] Or the dragon—being unintelligible or open to misunderstanding—is simply cut away, as in depictions of Catholic saints in Germany. Now these pictures show only the woman's bowed head, the object of her gaze having been removed. Or the dragon motif is simply omitted in stories of the lives of the saints.

The discovery of mythology in contemporary theology—and above all in feminist theology—allows the whole Martha picture to appear in a new light. Which unspoken traditions have shaped it? What unwritten traditions, traditions that are the expressions of faith contradicting the patriarchal traditions, lie behind it? From whence comes this mythological Martha tradition which is for us both alien and forgotten?

This Martha picture offers itself in both form and content to feminist research, first because the object of study is a woman who has been misjudged and unappreciated, second because it provokes an investigation of traditions which, mostly unwritten, are the traditions of minority groups, as found in art, folk and fairy tales, legends, and the history of religious life, the history of piety itself.

THE MARY-MARTHA SYMBOLS

In order to begin it is necessary that we investigate the picture of Martha as it is known and portrayed in the masculine, written history of theology. In so doing it will become clear that medieval theologians—like early Christian and contemporary theologians—were molded by the favorite contrast between the two sisters Mary and Martha; that is to say, they adopted the Lucan tradition (Luke 10). Mary embodies the life of contemplation (*vita contemplativa*), Martha the life of action (*vita activa*), whereby Mary enjoys spiritual priority. "The antithesis Mary-Martha is an undeniable characteristic of the medieval spiritual literature."[6]

Beginning with Origen and continuing with Augustine, Gregory the Great, Cassianus, monks like Norbert of Xanten, Bernard of Clairvaux, and many other medieval writers up to Luther, the New Testament story was made into a symbol of human life in which Martha played the least significant role. "Martha, Martha, your work must be brought to nothing," said Luther. Never has the Martha style of life been prized as useful and valuable in itself, not even by those who recognize and affirm the worth of an active life. The Martha *story* disappeared behind the dominating *symbol*.

THE MARTHA LEGEND

Against this background, the picture of the dragon-conquering Martha stands out in even richer contrast. This picture comes from a legend of Martha's victory over the dragon, and this legend comes from a thirteenth-century collection of legends gathered by the Dominican bishop Jacobus de Varagine.[7] From the mid-fourteenth century on, these legends were translated into the language of the people and were far more widely known than the Bible, which was officially available in Latin only since its translation into the mother tongue was continually forbidden. The legend collection was "the true book of the people of those times,"[8] as literature freely given and allowed, even recommended, by the clergy. It had a greater impact than the Bible of the ruling clergy on the piety of all social classes; in fact, it arose out of the "religion of the people."

The meager monotheism of Christianity, enriched by this collection, created in effect a Christian "Olympus." The Martha legend told how Martha, with her sister from Bethany, identified here as Mary Magdalene, and her brother Lazarus, was driven out of Palestine and traveled by ship to the south of France. There Martha preached and "was good of speech and pleasant for all"—an astonishing statement when one remembers that, according to some biblical texts, women should remain silent, and according to many contemporary commentators, Martha is too talkative. The people inhabiting the land between Arles and Avignon appealed to her for help. A human-eating dragon named Tarascus, "half-animal, half-fish, fatter than a steer and longer than a horse, with teeth like swords whose points are like horns," lay hidden in the Rhone River, killing everyone who crossed and sinking the ships. "Saint Martha went to oppose the dragon, for the people had asked her to. She found it in the forest eating someone. As soon as she poured holy water over it and held a cross in front of it, the dragon was subdued and stood there like a tame lamb. Martha bound it with her girdle. Then the people came and killed it with stones and spears." Later she became director of a nunnery and lived an ascetic life. A young man who wanted to hear her preach attempted to swim a river to reach her and drowned; she raised him from the dead. These astonishing legends about a woman with "masculine" traits must have arisen in the twelfth century, just before Martha's relics were discovered and veneration of her began at Tarascon in 1187.

In those stories elements of both biblical Martha stories appear with imaginative embellishment. Martha is hostess to Christ, and at the same time participates in the conquering of death by raising the dead man and capturing the dragon. The aspects of Martha judged by the patriarchal dogmatic tradition to be negative have now become fully positive features. Next to her sister Mary, whose story as the Magdalene legend had developed somewhat earlier, Martha was given her own highly esteemed capabilities, expressive

21

Jesus with Mary Magdalene and Martha

Martha Raising the Dead

of a fully developed character. The legends know nothing of a devaluing of her person, taking up again the Johannine tradition with mythological pictures.

The Dragon Motif

The dragon motif is the most interesting element of the Martha legends. Especially in France one can find—right up to the fashionable art of today (the church of Sacre Coeur!)—pictures of the missionary Saint Martha with the dragon. After the fifteenth century, when the legends were translated into German, the dragon continued, for a time, to be the typical distinguishing characteristic of Martha. Pictures of Martha with the dragon appeared in the fifteenth and sixteenth centuries in parts of Germany and in northern Italy. (There is an early depiction in the Catherine Chapel of the Strasbourg Cathedral, dating from 1350, corresponding to the Alsatian translation of the legend collection of 1336.) No iconology has yet recorded all such depictions. They come from great artists like Luini and Caravaggio and are also found on rural altars.

Where does this motif come from? Battle with a dragon is a theme found in all mythologies. A monster, either from land or from sea, that threatens the inhabitants of a city is known in the myths of almost all people. In most cases the dragon wants a sacrifice, often a virgin, but then the hero comes, frees the victim, and captures the dragon. Hercules saves Hesione this way in the Greek myth. In a transfer from Greek mythology to Christian legend, Saint George kills the dragon and thus rescues the king's daughter, who has been offered as the sacrifice. The king's daughter, Margarete, is also depicted as standing next to the dragon, which is bound with her girdle. But she belongs in the George legends from Asia Minor and is still the saved victim and not the victor herself.

In the Martha legends many elements of the dragon stories reappear. The dragon terrorizes a town and its inhabitants. Just like the rescued daughter of the king, Martha binds the dragon with her girdle and takes it to the town, where it is slain. The dragon, tamed by the woman's girdle, follows her like a lamb or a small pet. The new element in the Martha legend is that it is not a man here who is armored, armed, a hero, a soldier, who conquers this dragon; it

Martha Subduing a
Dragon

is a woman. Another new element is that the victory is friendly, without violence. Martha conquers the dragon by spiritual means, without weapons, without armor, and in bare feet and binds the dragon with her girdle, the sign of purity in a patriarchy and the symbol of eros and power in a matriarchy.

This dragon picture is fascinating because it is so contemporary. It is for some people in my country of Germany a political symbol: "Ohne Rüstung leben" ("To live without weapons"). The motif reaches back into pre-patriarchal concepts, appearing in the patriarchal culture of the Middle Ages like a relic of a long-outdated stage of civilization. In Egyptian art and mythology, which contain both patriarchal and matriarchal elements, one can encounter pictures of both women and men who tame water monsters, each according to her or his own style. Normally dragons are conquered by violence, now and again with tricks (for example, trapping them in a pit). In the Canaanite myth, Astarte asks Baal not to kill the dragon but to capture it instead. Furthermore, the assessment of the dragon depends on the level of consciousness of the day. In the matriarchal consciousness the dragon is a source of power which is in bondage; it represents elements that are unconscious, driving, and impassioned—all of which are positive and are to be integrated into human existence. The dragon or the snake belongs to the matriarchal goddess. It was her phallic symbol. It is her dark side and it is also the symbol of her wisdom. But the patriarchal consciousness regards the dragon as the driving force which is to be killed; in this case the same elements of power and passion are combined with the fear of women's power, the fear of anarchy and opposiion to the divine order. The snake or dragon is the symbol of the goddess which is to be overcome. To make it understandable for us personally, and to put it in modern terms, the dragon is what we fear and therefore hate and normally try to suppress. The other, nonviolent, way to get along with our fear is to integrate it, to accept it as part of our personality.

This wide variation in evaluating the dragon is also present in the Bible. In Job 41 Leviathan is a creature of God who belongs to creation even though it has a dark and dangerous as well as a charming side. In the book of Revelation the beast is clearly on the side of the antidivine and as such is a power to be overthrown.

Christianity became tied in general to the patriarchal Judeo-Roman culture. In the story of brave George the dragon-slayer, the dragon motif was taken up, and in this way Christianity identified itself with the patriarchal consciousness. Erich Neumann says, "Every patriarchal world is based on this titanic element . . . in which the motherly origin in the womb is banned into the underworld. Therefore the patriarchal world is proud to represent itself as the one who sets the foot on the head of the dragon from the deep."[9] The victory of a woman over the dragon, which is understood patriarchally as a satanic beast, appears in the Christian tradition again and again as the "woman whose foot crushes the head of the snake." But this patriarchal kick, which has been spread since the Counter-Reformation, is bound up with death and violence and has nothing to do with Martha. Saint Margaretha, whom we find now and again in a pose similar to Martha's, comes from another tradition. In any case, it is never reported that Martha conquered the dragon violently.

Here then is a unique mythology in which the power and spirituality of a woman is demonstrated. The Martha dragon myth integrates such pre-patriarchal images as the snake goddess and is therefore in a position to overcome the patriarchal consciousness in which rationality (embodied in the man) overcomes the irrational. A nonviolent way to get along with what we fear is shown. Here, in a Christian tradition, the picture of a divine woman with a dragon survived, while in all other cultures this original picture was distorted, as, for instance, the research of Edward Schaefer on Chinese culture shows.[10]

But the Christian hero, George the dragon-slayer, representing a somewhat older tradition, quickly overshadowed Martha and has remained the Christian symbol right up to the present. Even so, in Christian culture there is the Martha alternative, which was known and loved for centuries until it disappeared in the Reformation. In Tessin, however, there is still a depiction of Martha and the dragon from the eighteenth century.

MATRIARCHAL INFLUENCES

The origin of these dragon or similar motifs is not known, and until now no researcher has shown any interest in discovering it. I would like to make some suggestions.

First, there may have been influences from Egypt, where dragons, snakes, and crocodiles were regarded as holy and protected for much longer than in patriarchal cultures. Second, there is the possible influence of the spiritualist group called the Cathari, who joined together in southern France at the time the movement preaching absolute nonviolence arose. The picture of Martha in the legend— director of a nunnery, a woman preacher, an ascetic—corresponds to the attitudes of the Cathari concerning the possibilities for women. Conceivably the Cathari had feminine concepts of God. As with other Neoplatonic systems and various medieval sects, there may have been feminine emanations of the Deity such as Sapientia (Wisdom), Fides (Faith), and Justitia (Justice).[11] Third, the phenomenon of dragon-taming with holy incense is reminiscent of the great goddesses of the Mediterranean area who used the poppy as a drug. "The dragon that guarded the temple of the Hesperides was tamed by the priestess with the help of opium; the magical effect of the poppy was controlled by the woman."[12] The dragon-conquering Martha is reminiscent of the goddess cult in the ancient Mediterranean area.

A fourth possibility—which seems to me important and also never recognized before—is that the Martha tradition is connected to the Celtic cult of the mother deity. Just as the Celtic spring goddess Bridget was changed into the Saint Brigitte and the *Matres* (Mother) cult in southern France occurs again in the cult of the three Marys, it also appears that the Martha cult contains within it elements of a Celtic cult veneration of a goddess.

There are several reasons for saying this. First, according to the original French legend, retold in the nineteenth century by the Romantic poet Frédéric Mistral, Martha strikes water at a springhead. This is the typical function of a locally venerated Celtic spring goddess.[13]

Second, Martha's unusual way of dealing with the dragon is reminiscent of the goddess who, for a long time among the Celts, remained the mistress of the animals, birds, bears, and snakes. This shows, according to Erich Neumann, a matriarchal level of consciousness "in which the masculine ego had not yet begun [to dominate] with its own will, its consciousness, and its order of values. It becomes clear in the phenomenon of the human form of mistress of the animals that in nature the superior drive of feminine power is effective."[14] Snakes are found again and again in a trusting relationship with female deities.

Third, the word Martha, from a purely linguistic point of view, is linked with the surviving *Matres* or *Matrae* cults, which in the fifth century were already widespread and often integrated into Christian traditions. These cults were syncretistic venerations of three goddesses, a Celtic tradition supportive of women.[15] As with the veneration of Bridget, there are typical consonant changes. The French fairy tale "Maria Marte" likewise goes back to the mother cult. An old church prayer that begins "Ave Martha" was most likely originally "Ave Matre."

Fourth, an oft-recurring addition to the *Matres* cults is cake or bread. In accordance with these medieval concepts, Martha feeds with bread, whereas Mary feeds with milk.

Fifth, and finally, one of the oldest depictions of Martha—Martha at the grave of Lazarus, from the twelfth century, at Autun—shows Martha with neither bread nor dragon nor keys but instead with her arms raised and bent. According to Erich Jung, this is the posture of both blessing and ruling, taken mainly by goddesses and gods.[16]

A woman who derives her being from cosmic powers, who mediates, restrains, and tames these powers, who is not simply thought of as the birth-giving mother, seems to be the combination of the Martha and the *Matres* cults. For educational reasons the church allowed the cults of the saints to be founded on the sites of the other, older cults. That this takeover took a long time is not unusual. A *Matre* cult that had died out in one place would, with the discovery of holy stones, for example, become active again in the same place or would appear in another place.

THE DOMINICAN VENERATION OF MARTHA

How did the patriarchally shaped institutions of the church cope with the new Martha, who appeared so repeatedly in medieval art? The veneration of Mary the mother of Jesus, who continually brought the role of motherhood to the fore, was already established here; furthermore, there were also many female saints who provided a colorful pattern of feminine possibilities in the Middle Ages. But never had these female figures been as provocative as Martha.

Typical is the Dominican veneration of Martha. As Berthold Altaner has established, the Dominicans had a special relationship to Martha.[17] In the General Acts from 1264 to 1334, there are seven reminders to celebrate the Feast of Martha and to undertake organizing the day and the liturgy. At this time (1300) Meister Eckhart provocatively expounded on the Lucan Mary-Martha story for the first time. In the famous Mary-Martha sermon, Martha is the strong, active, successful, effective one; Mary is immature, vacillating, interested only in enjoyment and receiving. The charge of pantheism which was later leveled at Eckhart by the Inquisition can be seen in his picture of Martha: the woman broken by nothing; the one who works together with the cosmic powers. A further witness to the Dominican Martha piety is the Dominican preacher and mystic Venturino of Bergamo (1304-46), who founded the Martha cloister, a Reformed cloister with a new alternative life-style.[18] A third witness to the Dominican veneration of Martha is the fifteenth-century Florentine painter Fra Angelico. Above an abbey cell in San Marco he painted the Garden of Gethsemane on the night of Jesus' arrest; next to the sleeping men Peter, James and John he placed two women awake: Mary and Martha. This was a blunt way of dealing with tradition and a strong provocation to the church founded on Peter. Martha is praying like Christ; she conforms exactly to him. And in a crucifixion scene, *Martha* stands next to Christ.

The cause for this special relationship to Martha seems to be bound closely to the development of the Dominican order itself. The order was founded by Dominic as a begging and preaching order with the aim of opposing the Cathari movement in southern France. The Cathari were a protest against the church hierarchy. They also allowed women into higher positions within their movement. The women's movement of the twelfth century found a new richness and new possibilities with the Cathari. "This heresy cleared a free and independent place for women within their community."[19]

Among women Dominic also began to oppose heresy. At Prouille in 1206, he founded a nunnery consisting of women "who were previously followers of the dualists."[20] The southern French veneration of Martha was centered in Tarascon and the Dominican

Prouille. We can suppose that the French women were familiar with the Martha cult, her legend, and her veneration. We can also suppose that the Dominicans combined their biblicism and their catholicity with the image of Martha, and from then on the veneration of Martha found a secure place among the Dominicans.

Nevertheless, Martha of Tarascon also had heretical features: she preached. She did not fit the world of the cloister which, as in Prouille, was under masculine rule and spiritual guidance. Presumably the Dominicans dealt cleverly with these features. Her preaching, her dragon-conquering, and her act of raising from the dead do not appear in the Dominican concept, although the legend, as Eckhart shows, was known. Martha was domesticated and placed in the role of hostess to Christ. Since the Dominican women's cloisters were a church-controlled channel for the medieval women's movement, the Dominicans guided the picture of Martha into a patriarchally suited bed. Even so, because of Meister Eckhart and Fra Angelico, there appears for women a new model of a self-aware, self-reliant co-worker of Christ and partner of God.

The Martha Cult and Martha Institutions

Although the Martha cult was widespread in the Middle Ages, above all in southern Germany, France, and Italy, it never experienced the dimensions and claims of the Mary cult. Because of this it has clearly retained its own identity, which mediates an independent, positive, and successful picture of woman, neither bound by motherhood like Mary nor denigrated by sin like Magdalene. The cult was maintained largely in fringe groups. In the main church, where the image of woman was dominated either by mother or by sinner, it had less success. There the Mary-mother-virgin figure overshadowed Martha, who represents the other side of women—the older, mature, independent person—that disappeared more and more in the process of patriarchalization, as did the threefold matriarchal goddesses in other patriarchalized religions.

Parallels to the veneration of Mary are found in the following images. Like Mary, Martha is also *juber coeli, rosa mundi* ("light of heaven, rose of earth").[21] Like the protective mantle of Mary, Martha's protective mantle in the Martha church in Carona (Tessin)

31

was extended over those who venerated her. All these images go back to pagan goddesses and were extended to Martha as well as Mary. They are therefore not transfers from Mary to Martha.

Similar to Martha but different from her are the following pictures. Jesus goes into the house of Martha as into the womb of Mary (Bernard of Clairvaux). As Mary feeds Jesus with milk, so Martha feeds him with bread (*Halberstadt Breviery* of 1510):

> Sicut sacrato ubere
> virgo Christum ablactavit
> sic Martha saluti fere
> suis cibi ipsum parit.

> As from her sacred breast
> Christ the Virgin fed with milk,
> Martha brings salvation so:
> with food she has herself prepared.

In contrast to Mary, Martha is a self-reliant, integrated, "together" woman who provides good food, who is a hostess who opens her house, and whose existence as a woman is not defined by her sexual organs. (This corresponds to the ideas of a contemporary woman I heard recently: "Martha has always been totally great and strong for me; Mary, small and wholly tender.") Martha is a strong woman. She is like a goddess who brings help. She brings salvation (*saluti fere*). Her story does not allow her to be reduced by sexuality, devaluation of the body, or similar patriarchal distortion—like Mary and Magdalene. Her medieval picture reminds us today of the type of a matriarchal goddess who is mistress of the animals, fertility, and the underworld and has resurrection power. The key she sometimes wears is not only the household key, but also the key to the underworld.

Between 1200 and 1500, church institutions like Guilds, hospitals, and women's cloisters were founded in the name of this Martha. Along with these also arose the Martha churches, which have been preserved until now. All these were animated by the Martha legend but not all have survived the Middle Ages.

The most interesting institutions were the Martha cloisters in Italy founded by Venturino of Bergamo. They offered an alternative lifestyle by which they distinguished themselves from the growing luxury that was coming into fashion; simple clothes and abstinence from meat, cheese, eggs, and wine, as in the Martha legend. In contrast to the women's cloisters up to that time, the language of the people was cultivated and well-spoken, especially in the liturgy. In the name of Martha, Venturino also recommended to the Dominicans and others who did not belong to the cloister the use of the Bible and the liturgy in the mother tongue. This was a kind of revolution.

Perhaps this trend is reflected in the minutes of the Inquisition from the fourteenth century where various sources give the name "Martha" to spiritual directors of convents who were suspected of being heretical.[22] There are corresponding reports for the abbeys of the Brothers of the Common Life. The few witnesses from whom we have written accounts are enough to show that Martha became a symbol for religious reform and because of this was pushed to the edge of heresy.

The Martha cloisters of modern times are unambiguously institutions with practical aims, above all, care of the sick. The Martha houses of nineteenth-century Protestantism were houses of deaconesses designed for service. Today Martha is the patroness of the cooks and housekeepers of Catholic clergy, and an antiemancipation movement in England bears her name. Martha has again been domesticated and ordered according to sex. After her short awakening in the Middle Ages, she has been integrated into the patriarchal church and society.

Martha was a female figure seen by the early church in close relationship to Jesus and to the resurrection. Subsequently, the patriarchal culture of the church assigned her a fixed, sex-specific role— serving—and in that role she has come down to us in tradition.

In the Bible of the "little people," in minority groups, and in the medieval legends about Martha, the original significance of this woman comes to life in an up-to-date way. Through Martha's victory over the dragon, matriarchal elements that shaped the "religion of the people" in the Middle Ages again emerged. At the same time the legend confirms that in the medieval women's movement women did engage in such "spiritual" activities as public preaching.

In the long run the church was not able to cope with the picture of a woman with authority not defined by men, with cosmic powers sovereign over the forces of the abyss, and who exercised divine functions. The church excluded that image. The dominant picture of woman became Mary, mother and virgin, and this arrested all attempts to retain the matriarchal women's heritage and to foster a permanent tradition expressive of woman's worth as such.

Church history shows that the development of a centralized church with a hierarchy has constantly gone together with an emphasis on Mary as mother and virgin. In contrast to this, the pluralistic churches have coped with many different women's traditions. The patriarchalization of our Christian heritage was made complete by the appearance of a dominant church tradition. This patriarchalization is not, however, necessarily bound to the Christian message, and in the courts of history it has been and can be broken through again and again.

In the symbolic image of the female victory over the dragon, concepts which have long been depreciated by the church (such as the reconciliation of spirit and body, and reconciliation with the snake) can become vital again and express our contemporary relationship with nature, the psyche, and the irrational. Even reconciliation with what seems as foreign and hostile to us as the dragon (e.g., nations, enemies, strangers), becomes in the picture of Martha and the dragon a model of hope. Behind the patriarchalization of the Christian tradition—and here I oppose Mary Daly's thesis in *Beyond God the Father*[23]—there is visible a matriarchal Christian subculture. Therefore, waiting behind the patriarchal facade are pictures and symbols that carry in themselves the original liberating power of the gospel, even for today.

3

Christianity Between Patriarchy and Matriarchy

Today we Christians are confronted with a remarkable phenomenon. For centuries Christianity has been a great wellspring of freedom for women, as well as the source of great women's liberation movements. The American women's movement of the last century based itself on Christian principles of human rights, thereby affecting the European women's rights movement. The radical demand for individual rights is also one of the roots of today's feminist movement. Nevertheless, women presently experience a Christianity that has, with its church and through its theology, decisively contributed toward the development of a destructively intolerant patriarchal society.

Research has demonstrated that Judeo-Christian religion evolved and came to prevail within the framework of a patriarchal society, destroying and disparaging elements of an earlier matriarchal culture. We must ask ourselves whether this marriage between our Christian tradition and patriarchy is as indissoluble as Mary Daly claims[1] and as Karl Barth confirms it, saying, "The Bible in fact presupposes as the earthly and temporal order of the relationship of man and woman not the matriarchy but the patriarchy."[2] Are women then left with the alternative of abandoning Christianity entirely?

The recovery of a matriarchal heritage is a fascinating prospect—for men as well as for women—because it not only illuminates a long-obscure system of values and order, but also spotlights the patriarchal deficiency. It is a widespread patriarchal error that in matriarchy the strong mother took the place of the strong father. Matriarchy—as research shows from John Jacob Bachofen until today—is a brotherly-sisterly society, quite different from patriarchy. It is a source of democracy, Bachofen says, and it gives us today the only model of what a woman might be if not defined by man in a male society.[3]

What makes matriarchy so fascinating for women today? In a matriarchy women belong to the propertied class and can inherit. They can serve as clergy, and in addition to that decisively religious function are also protectors of the arts and sciences. In a matriarchy the body and nature are not subjugated, but integrated, and sensuality and sexuality are not repressed, but tamed, for it is the goddess who is mistress of the animals. In a matriarchy an uninhibited sociability, free of repression, makes peaceful coexistence between men and women, children and adults, and different tribes possible. On Crete, for example, where archaeological evidence shows a comprehensive reconstruction of a matriarchal culture, one has yet to uncover weapons of any kind.

Furthermore, one should not hesitate to take into account what may at first appear to be an invitation to self-deception. The myth of the matriarchy has a long and rich tradition and holds a certain fascination, even for men.[4] It is essentially something quite real, as demonstrated by anthropological research. In any case, beneath the matriarchy of history lies a matriarchy of psychic dimensions: the yearning for a deeper harmony with all that is, beyond all patriarchal estrangement; the search for the happiness that we miss in our society: a dream that looks behind us and contradicts our understanding of reason and reality, yet a dream that can mobilize hope and creativity to change. Women today live between the matriarchy that they dream of and the patriarchy they suffer under and ask how Christianity relates to these cultures.

I would like to investigate two questions: (1) How can we explain

36

the fact that Christianity was for so long a primary source of freedom for women, while at the same time it allowed a patriarchal theology and culture to develop? (2) Are there any hidden matriarchal elements in Christianity that have managed to survive its patriarchal structuring and that may have accompanied or even precipitated women's movements in the past?

The Patriarchalization of the Gospel

The common origin of Christianity and women's rights movements lies in the gospel of freedom, equality, and emancipation of all people through Jesus. We know Jesus as the leader of a nonascetic, charismatic, itinerant movement. Men and women followed this wandering preacher who told of the coming of the kingdom of God, which would precipitate a transformation of all social and personal values. This movement did not stress self-denial and penitence as with John the Baptist, nor was it limited only to men, as in Qumran.

We know from the stories about Jesus that he was by no means an ascetic but joyfully took part in feasts and celebrations. He particularly addressed himself to the many peripheral groups, and more than anything associated himself with women in a partnerlike manner. To the surprise and frustration of his closest male friends, he was known even to prefer the company of women, and there is nothing in the tradition that tells of his ever having been angry with a woman.[5] Within the congregations formed after his death, there were handed down stories that reflect the impartial and socially revolutionary dimensions of this movement.

Two aspects of these stories especially attract attention today. First, Jesus liberated women from their former social roles, out of family bonds. Speaking to each of them individually, he helped them become individuals. One thinks of Joanna, the wife of a royal minister of finance, who leaves her husband; her dramatic story was kept away from Christian women, who had to be obedient to their husbands. In Luke 24 she, with Mary Magdalene, is told to tell the disciples about the resurrection of Jesus. Or one thinks of Salome, mother of the disciples James and John, who unlike her sons did not flee when Jesus was taken prisoner but remained and stood beneath the cross. In our family-oriented churches we have forgot-

37

ten that the gospel primarily helps people—both male and female—become individuals and gives them the necessary courage.

Second, Jesus broke with the taboos that surrounded Eastern women. He accepted women as they were, even though their bodies were considered weak and unclean in his culture, the reason they were not allowed to take part in the cult. He healed a hemorrhaging woman and, according to the custom of his day, became unclean himself by touching her. He raised Jairus' daughter, holding her hand. Yet he did not touch the men that he raised from the dead. Through a Christianity that for the most part has been reduced to soul and spirit, people have come to be out of touch with (if not calloused to) all the sensual dimensions of the gospel.

We Christians can no longer afford to ignore the fact that women were the only ones who did not flee when Jesus was taken captive. Of his intimate friends, they were the only ones to stand beneath the cross. They were present at his burial, and they were the first witnesses of his resurrection. It is the women who are recognized as the actual bearers of the tradition of Jesus' death and resurrection. The early charismatically organized congregations reflect this privileged status of women, much to the amazement of their environment. Women could lead congregations and were apostles and bishops. In the diverse cultures of the ancient world, women could become independent businesspersons, enjoying great freedom and respect. But I must agree with Hanna Wolff, who regards Jesus as the first to overcome the androcentrism of the ancient world, that this never had any lasting social impact. In the person and history of Jesus, the traditional animosity toward women was suspended. In fact, he had himself personally integrated so many male and female behavioral characteristics that one could consider him the first maturely integrated person. This made history. It called into being movements that stretch from ancient times into the present. Where founders of great religions had been open to women, this factor never had any measurable social impact before Jesus. Whenever women appealed to their rights during the following 1,900 years, whenever they thought of themselves as being integral human beings, they understood themselves to be acting in harmony with the Jesus movement. The feminism that shines out of the Gospels motivated the majority of them, even though they found no support in the church. A Korean woman today writes: "Jesus may have emancipated women

2,000 years ago, but men still cite only those Bible passages that suit them."

There is one problem that we Christians have yet to come to terms with. One could ask, and rightly so, how such integrated congregations could produce the rule that women should keep silent in church? How could such a revolutionary atmosphere produce such discriminatory words as these: that a woman should keep silent; that she will be blessed through her children but her husband through his faith; and that the woman was the first to sin, and then induced her husband to sin?

The answer is that the gospel has been handed down to us in a patriarchal form. I see three stages of patriarchalization. (1) The Bible itself has undergone a patriarchal editing. (2) Throughout the Western world, the Bible has been received in a patriarchal manner. (3) Even today the Bible is being patriarchally translated, interpreted, and preached.

An example of patriarchal editing of the Bible is the famous command that women should keep silent in the churches. It is in Paul's first letter to the Corinthians, but it does not appear to come from Paul himself, for it contradicts the congregational practice of the apostle (a third of whose colleagues were female), as well as his theology: "There is neither Jew nor Greek, . . . male nor female; for you are all one in Christ Jesus [Gal. 3:28]." The admonition appears to have originated at a time when the leadership of the church was firmly in the hands of men, and women had again been silenced. In the Gospels we are acquainted with women who are tough and intelligent debaters, for example, Martha, who argues with Jesus until he raises Lazarus from the dead, and then, in a manner very similar to Peter, confesses that Jesus is the Christ (John 11:27).

A good illustration of the patriarchal reception of the Bible is the fate of Mary Magdalene, who is generally known only as the "great sinner." She was, however, not a prostitute but an intimate friend of Jesus whom he had healed from mental illness. After their meeting on Easter morning she became the first to tell of his resurrection. The male administration of the church apparently had a difficult time coping with this, and as the Western world began to translate sin in terms of body and sexuality, "man" (especially Augustine) learned to project his conflicts onto the figure of a woman. The story of Mary Magdalene (Luke 8:2) was combined with the story of the great sinner (Luke 7:36-50), and out of that came the picture of Mary Magdalene the sexual sinner which has left such an impression on literature, liturgy, and the arts.

Even today the Bible is being patriarchally interpreted, as translations, commentaries, and sermons demonstrate. We have, for example, Phoebe, who is ranked as a "deaconess," even though she performed the duties of a bishop. Or the female apostle Junia, who is always transformed into the male apostle Junias (Romans 16:6). Identified with a world limited to love and emotions, women are delegated corresponding duties, such as nursing or charity work. But if Jesus himself came to serve in a similar manner, and if we are all to imitate him, it should follow that no duties be limited to a particular sex.

With these three patriarchal estrangements in the gospel, women were once again relegated to the confines of the family: they were understood in a one-sided manner, only in terms of their role in the family. Consequently, they were turned into sex objects and made the very image of weakness and sin.

The patriarchal tradition forms a kind of double-ballast for women to drag around. This hierarchical way of thinking, which ties women to particular "female" duties, impedes democratic progress even within the family circle. Furthermore, it brings with it an alienation from physical nature that makes it difficult for women today to experience the whole person (body, soul, and spirit), to develop male and female possibilities of a more mature nature, and to accept our physical bodies along with all their repressed wishes and instincts.

MATRIARCHAL ELEMENTS WITHIN CHRISTIANITY

The Christian faith suffocates within the prison of its patriarchal thought-structure. But are there matriarchal elements in it that we can turn to today; matriarchal elements that bring the wholeness of woman closer to us? Have things been said about women, nature, and society that might have originally come out of a matriarchal context and with which women today might identify? These questions can be asked now that women have begun to uncover their own history, *her*-story, and have become conscious of the heritage around them that has been obscured.

Judeo-Christian religion was from the beginning surrounded by matriarchal or semimatriarchal religions. In the Europe of the Middle Ages, Christianity came into contact with a strongly matriarchal Celtic religiosity, the impact of which was felt in southern France and Ireland as late as the sixteenth century. But has any of this had a lasting impact? If so, what kinds of psychic forces were unleashed? What kinds of creativity were stimulated? Did these lead to the integration of any eternal universal visions? And what meaning did all this have for female consciousness?

It is my opinion that several matriarchal elements form a fundamental part of the Judeo-Christian religion, but we must first learn to discern and differentiate them. We must learn especially how to discover new dimensions for our theological thinking. Three things are important.

To begin with, writing, education, science, and religion have developed in a patriarchal context. The Judeo-Christian religion is tied to a book that was written down by men, who thereby introduced the perspective and interests of the dominant male class. Since written theology has until now been able to produce only a distorted and inadequate picture of women and their relationships, we must regard the written tradition of the Judeo-Christian faith— Old Testament, New Testament, canon law, and dogmatics—as biased and inadequate sources. Matriarchal images or modes of thinking are present only unconsciously or peripherally.

Second, the value of written religion has often been overrated. Fascinated by what is for them a newly discovered science, women have often come to regard it as the only source of religion, thereby becoming trapped in male behavior patterns. However, alongside the written religion there is also a religion of experience that is far more difficult to grasp than the written religion and has received little attention. The history of piety, culture, and art in religion is nevertheless an important area from which a "religion" could be reconstructed. In order to comprehend the whole reality of religion and not just the part that has been written down, one should examine works of art and other documents of piety.

Third, in addition to the written tradition and artistic expression there also exists a narrative tradition, which is even more difficult

41

to grasp. We can detect this tradition in legends of the Middle Ages, for example, where with much fantasy and in an unconventional manner both pagan and biblical images come alive and are expanded on. Many have had their faith conveyed to them by means of a narrative tradition that often bears a striking contrast to the official religion. One finds here a reflection of a tradition of mothers, with its own imaginative language or images. And it is here, for example, that mothers refrain from introducing their children to a "Lord" God or the "man" Jesus, but try to convey through the sensitive language and pictures of their own religious experience a sense of identity and freedom.

If we examine religion from this more universal perspective, we stand a better chance of coming closer to the reality of religious life, the reality of people, and most of all the reality of women. Then a subculture becomes tangible that can be compared with the dominant culture. People become sensitized to matriarchal elements that appear, are cherished, and passed down.

Example 1: The Old Testament. At first glance the Yahweh religion seems to have radically cut itself off from all matriarchal cults. With the immigration of the patriarchal tribes into Palestine, the Yahweh religion was able to develop and make its mark on the then still matriarchally structured Mediterranean world, overcoming and replacing the old religion. According to today's matriarchal research, the Old Testament is a classic example of a patriarchal religion in which the transition from an old matriarchal religion into a patriarchal religion is complete.[6] Yahweh has managed to absorb all the characteristics of the goddess, as he is also female in a motherly way, in that he gives birth, acts as housekeeper, and so on.

The Levitical laws of the Old Testament originated with a tribe that was part of the Indo-Germanic patriarchal immigration, a tribe that seems to have forced a patriarchalization. The law may have required the protection of widows and orphans (Exodus 22:22), but otherwise women were treated as property (Exodus 21:22; 22:16). While the manumission of male slaves was legal, fathers could sell their own daughters as slaves (Exodus 21:1-7). But the old religion remained quite alive among the people, and the prophets' protests against the fertility cults reflect the long, hard struggle that this new patriarchal religion fought against, the old matriarchal religion. The bearers of these cults appear to have been for the most part women, coming from within a subdued matriarchally organized population.

Three elements of eschatological hope appear to have originated within a matriarchal context: (1) "The land of milk and honey" is a matriarchal conception. Honey is the product of a bee colony, an organization where a woman rules, while milk is the basic means of subsistence and comes from a mother. (2) In Isaiah we find the concept that in the peace at the end of time "the sucking child shall play over the hole of the asp, and weaned child shall put his hand on the adder's den [Isa. 11:8]." The snake is a symbol of the goddess who in patriarchal thinking had become a dangerous, tempting, and evil animal. At the end of time, however, she should once again become the companion of humans. (3) Jeremiah 31:22 speaks of the expectation that the woman shall at some time in the future again become the protector of man.

These images are the clearest repository for the dreams and memories of humankind, especially of women. All cultures are conscious of the visionary power of women. Visionary power is especially present in oppressed cultures, whereby a spirituality of the oppressed becomes possible. These collective memories direct themselves toward a bygone age, where the snake, the female, and vegetable foods determined a system of values. They are the expression of a matriarchal subculture, one that has managed to make room for itself within the dominating culture, where it was able to impress itself on eschatological hope. A marginal subculture can therefore be read out of the Old Testament itself. Figures like Miriam (who was originally not the sister of Moses but an independent leader of the tribes of Israel during the Exodus), as well as Deborah and Jael, provide evidence of an earlier female culture. There is, in fact, a whole tradition of women's songs that stretches throughout the Old Testament in connection with names like Judith, Hannah, Deborah, Jael, and Miriam—all contradicting a patriarchal religion that puts God on the side of everything that is strong and male and witnessing to a different experience of God, one that does not quite fit into the dominating structure of patriarchal piety.

Example 2: The Middle Ages. If one examines the research done on the subject of women in the Middle Ages—that is, research working exclusively out of patriarchal sources—one often comes across restrictive laws that had been passed against women (the Gratian decrees), as well as evidence of defensive struggles of the church throughout Europe against a rising women's movement. It is claimed, for instance, that women were strictly forbidden to preach, but if one approaches the subject using different sources, an entirely different picture of female life in the Middle Ages becomes visible.

The motif of Martha the dragon-conqueror, for example, originated in twelfth-century France and became more common as it accompanied the women's movements of the Cathari and Waldensians, remaining popular until the Reformation. It is possible that the legend was originally cherished in convents and subsequently found its way into the wider stream of general piety. This picture, which Christian iconography has almost completely neglected, represents the forgotten goddess—the integrated woman—in a Christianity that was generally so patriarchally oriented. The way Martha tames the dragon with her girdle reminds us of the matriarchal mistress of the animals and her cosmic power. Even the most famous painters of the Middle Ages chose to depict her, yet it remained a motif of a subculture. The motif that was to prevail was that of "George the Dragon-slayer," because it conformed to the patriarchal concept of life and the world.

The twelfth century saw not only papal sanction of the concept of Mary Magdalene as the "great sinner," but also production (stimulated by legends familiar in southern France) of paintings and stained-glass windows with Mary Magdalene depicted as a priestess and preacher. If we examine well-known sources of the history of the church during this period, there is nothing that would point to a female culture that might conform to this artistic tradition. Our attention having been caught by the frequency of this motif during this period, we are surprised to find that women are often forbidden to preach. The conclusion follows that there *were* women preaching during the Middle Ages, but that our written patriarchal tradition was content to ignore it. This is yet another clue to the existence of a female subculture that has not yet been fully grasped: a subculture that claimed to represent the priestess of the forgotten goddess—that is to say, to represent the total, integral, and independent woman of Christianity.

In several medieval descriptions of women, one comes across a matriarchal pattern that does not seem to have been touched by

44

Anna Selbdritt. The Christian version of the original matriarchal Trinity.

patriarchal disparagement of women. The female trinity "Anna Selb-dritt" is a repetition of the classic matriarchal picture of Kore, Demeter, and Erechtheus. The motif of the crying woman, an image that does not appear in the Bible in this way, is a primary component of the matriarchal as well as the medieval description of women: the goddess who laments the loss of her hero. "The Virgin that opened herself," a figure of Mary that one could open and find God the Father and Jesus, was forbidden as heretical but nevertheless remained a favorite medieval image and can be traced back to the conception of Mother Nature.

Example 3: The seventeenth century. After the Thirty Years War a princess of Württemberg commissioned the painting of an altarpiece that depicted a matriarchal view of Christian salvation. Stimulated by the Jewish mysticism of the Kabbala, she found the courage to express her own religious experience and conception of salvation in the commission of these paintings in a Black Forest church.

If one examines them carefully, these paintings are quite challenging to traditional beliefs. The outer wings depict ninety-four female figures from the Bible—and not a single man—as they approach Christ. Opening the wings, one sees the princess herself, watching the process of salvation from her own perspective. She is in a garden with many plants that can be precisely identified. Biblical figures, patriarchs, and prophets are also shown. The whole piece is crowned with a cupola, in the shadowy background of which the trinity of Father, Son, and Holy Spirit is depicted, while the center clearly depicts a female trinity in bright colors.[7] Like the creation goddess, the female "Holy Spirit" has in her hand a snake, the old symbol for the matriarchal unity of earth, life, wisdom, salvation, and women. This is not merely a female element that has been added to a male trinity, in itself a frequent phenomenon. A matriarchal transformation of religious experience has taken place here, and it was tolerated and has remained intact.

Example 4: The twentieth century. For an example from the twentieth century, I would like to use a personal story. My first experience with Jesus was that Jesus was female. Perhaps this is the reason I never had a problem that Jesus was a man. My mother had always spoken to me of Jesus as the *Christkind* coming at Christ-

46

The Snake-goddess of Crete

Kether, Chockma, and Bina—Three female images of the Trinity.

mastime to earth, a figure coming out of poetry with fair hair and in a long gown. Recently I read that this *Christkind* is a remnant of the Germanic goddess Freya, or Frau Holle, who visits children in wintertime.[8] So my mother—although educated by her Prussian pastor father in a conservative Christian way—used a matriarchal picture with which she, and her daughter, could identify. By means of friendly matriarchal elements, this narrative tradition brought the gospel of freedom and identity into my strongly patriarchal world.

THE MATRIARCHAL SUBCULTURE AS RESOURCE FOR RENEWAL

Without forgetting the negative pictures of women that limit a woman to the humble roles of either mother or virgin, I think that matriarchal images, fantasies, and dreams have demonstrated an extraordinary vitality. They were consistently sustained by lively matriarchal memories and the claim that women were integral personalities.[9] Nevertheless, many women were attacked, accused of heresy, and even burned.

In order to uncover the history of women, it is not enough merely to discover female elements in a religion that has been patriarchally dominated. These elements serve only to illustrate the painful process of transformation from a matriarchal religion to a patriarchal religion. Neither is it sufficient to expose a counterculture, thereby perhaps even conjuring one up. Feminist research is often confronted with countercultures that have been destroyed, for example, the culture of witches, now continued in the goddess movement. It seems to me that prevailing elements of a matriarchal subculture have been ignored here, elements that reflect the Christian woman's own experience with freedom and that we women have failed to integrate. Although ignored, this subculture remains neither assimilated nor obliterated and is in many ways comparable to the spirituality of blacks.

Alongside the patriarchalization of the Gospels, we are able to ascertain remnants of the matriarchal subculture. In its statements about the integral dignity and essential completeness of women, as well as about nature and the necessity for a more natural sociability beyond all oppression, this female motif is able to express the gospel much better than comparable patriarchal statements about women, nature, and society. Within this subculture it has been possible for people, especially women, to survive the unhealthy, suffocating narrowness of the church's patriarchal structure. But this subculture must first be uncovered in its entire historical breadth.

Matriarchal modes of thought have preserved such basic human values as the self-reliant function of women; the integration of nature, the body, and sensuality; and the dream of a cosmic world of freedom. These are values that had been nearly obliterated by a patriarchal craving for domination.

Christianity, however, transcends all patriarchal and matriarchal categories. Both men and women can inherit, not just the men as in the patriarchy and not just the woman's family as in the matriarchy. Both have visions, are one in Christ, and are not fixed in certain sexual roles. Christianity provides identity and at the same time transcends the search for identity in that it challenges an ever-changing world to provide more justice and freedom for all.

The subculture must be uncovered and listened to as an alternative to the dominating culture. This need applies to the scholarly world as well as to our present Christian culture, which is still so strongly patriarchal. Engaging in this task means letting fantasy have a legitimate place alongside dogmatics, experience alongside our written heritage. It means a rediscovery of the Holy Spirit not only as dogma, but in practice. In concrete terms it means recognizing that women have a right to speak, to let their imaginations be felt, and to share responsibility in the churches and in theology.

Jürgen Moltmann

GOD WITH THE HUMAN FACE

BRIEF EXPLANATION OF
ILLUSTRATIONS

Page 72—The medieval mystic Hildegard of Bingen views the divine Trinity in the perfection of a circle. Like rays streaming from the sun, the Holy Spirit in the form of a woman steps forth from the circle of the Father and the circle of the Son, with hands raised in blessing.

Page 79—In the Middle Ages the central form for representing the triune God was the "Seat of Grace." One recognizes immediately that the Trinity has at its center the death of Christ on the cross and is revealed in the Crucified One. The doctrine of the Trinity and the theology of the cross are united in this picture. The Holy Spirit descends in the form of the dove from the Father on the dead Son in order to resurrect him.

Page 85—Andrei Rubljov painted the best-known and most famous Russian icon around 1415 for the Church of the Trinity in Sagorsk. It depicts the Trinity in the form of three angels, who, according to Genesis 18, appeared to Abraham and Sarah by the oaks of Mamre. Rubljov has left Abraham and Sarah out and has represented the Trinity in intimate conversation. I believe the angel in the middle represents God the Father, for the movement of the three persons proceeds from him. The angel on the left represents the Holy Spirit, who receives a glance from the Father and points with his hand to the Son, who sits on the right, and blesses him. At stake is the sending of the Son on the way of suffering for the reconciliation of the world. For this reason the chalice stands in the middle. The coordination of the hands of the three Persons depicts the Trinity open to the sacrifice of love. Also in this picture the doctrine of the Trinity and the theology of the cross are united.

Page 86—Pictures of the Pietà have been known generally since the beginning of the thirteenth century. In place of the enthroned Mary with the king of the world on her knee, as in the romanesque period, the poor, pain-wracked, sorrowful mother with the dead and battered son is presented.

Page 87—Less well known are the corresponding pictures in which God the Father is represented with the dead Son in his arms. They are shaped often in parallel ways and similarly constructed. Yet the look of the Father expresses not so much sympathy and pain, but much more the sense of the delivering up of the Son to the death on the cross, the complete sacrifice of reconciliation. Whoever sees the Father should know *why* the Son suffered this death in Godforsakeness.

Page 99—The Seat of Grace/Trinity picture from Naples depicts the Father, not decisive and triumphant, but rather with the expression of deep pain on his face. Here the Son seems to reflect on his peaceful face the feeling of victory: "It is accomplished."

Page 102—The Trinity with the female Holy Spirit between the Son and the Father comes from the Middle Ages and is to be found in the village church in Urschalling, in Bavaria. It is, so far as I know, unique and has been preserved only in this out-of-the-way place in the church.

Page 105—The Seat of Grace/Trinity picture of El Greco shows the Crucified One without the cross as he is brought back by the angel into the arms of the eternal Father. The Holy Spirit hovers as a dove over the Son and the Father, presumably in order to proclaim the day of the new creation that begins with the resurrection of the dead Son of God.

4

God Means Freedom

The title "God Means Freedom" immediately provokes two questions: Does God in all the divine majesty really mean freedom for us human beings? And if so, what kind of freedom do we experience in God's presence?

GOD AND FREEDOM

No one seems to like the combination God *and* freedom. Neither some of the pious nor atheists are for the slogans "God *and* freedom" and "Freedom *and* God." Some of the pious are anxious about freedom. They say that freedom destroys the authority of the state, freedom dissolves the family bond, freedom shatters the moral law, and too much freedom drives first men and now women out of the church. Thus, they argue, whatever begins in the name of freedom always ends in terror and chaos.

Atheists, however, would ban God from freedom. Either there

is a God—and then humanity is not free, they contend—or humanity is free, and then there can be no God. The pious Dostoyevsky feared, "If there were no God, then everything would be permitted." The atheist Jean-Paul Sartre responded seventy years later, "But everything is permitted; people are totally free. Therefore, there is no God."[1]

For many people in Europe since the French Revolution, the command is not to seek God *and* freedom but simply to choose between God and freedom. God *or* freedom? That is the question, they say. If I believe in God, then I obligate myself to obey the moral code and the dogma of the church. It follows that I am not free, but tied down. But if I want freedom, then I must break all bonds, take my life in my own hands, and accept responsibility for all the things I do and also for all the things I believe. If I believe in the authority of God, I am in addition bound to recognize the earthly authority of the family, the church, and the state. But if I believe in the power of freedom, then I should recognize no authority other than freedom alone and my own decision, wherever it leads me. "*Ni Dieu—ni maître*," cried the freedom-fighters of the French Revolution. "Neither God nor state," said graffitti of anarchists at Tübingen's *Stiftskirche* recently.[2]

When one thinks of the alternative God or freedom, atheism is the logical presupposition for liberation from economic, political, cultural, and religious dependence. Then atheism and not religion becomes the fundamental postulate of the citizen come of age, the free man and the free woman. In Europe this has been asserted not only by such revolutionary thinkers as Karl Marx, Mikhail Bakunin, and Nikolai Lenin, but also by such philosophical moralists as Friedrich Nietzsche and Nicolai Hartmann.

Not the "praying hands" in the church—remember the famous picture by Albrecht Dürer hanging on the walls of many pious homes—but the raised clenched fist on the street has become the symbol of the will to freedom everywhere in the world today. Who belongs on the saint's calendar? asked Karl Marx. Christ or Prometheus? The servant of God or the rebel against the gods? And he placed Prometheus as his own saint on the calendar of the revolution.[3] Thus it has remained in many European countries until today: God or freedom? Freedom or God? This is the question.

But is this really the question? Isn't this alternative deceptive and false? Let us look at this question in the historical perspective. With the rise of the political and national revolutions of the nineteenth century, many freedom-fighters (e.g., the Forty-eighters) understood Christianity as "the religion of freedom." For them, faith was the courage to found a new community of people without privileges. They did not want to destroy religion; they wanted to use it to liberate humanity to its higher potentialities. They dreamed of a free church in a free state. The Christian religion strengthened in them the eschatological hope for the future kingdom where freedom reigns.

But for the most part since the French Revolution, the churches in Europe—both Catholic and Protestant—have made a holy alliance with the reactionary powers, which was really unholy. Conservative theologians could see only original sin in the liberation movements of the citizens. Therefore they regarded original sin as rebellion against God—and censured every rebellion. They depreciated the emancipation of slaves, of women, and of the proletariat as "falling away from God." They turned the dream—also the "American Dream"—of a realm of freedom, open to all, into a nightmare of an authoritarian religion for "God, king, fatherland," or for "family, God, and fatherland."[4] Since then, in many European countries and former European colonies in Latin America and Africa, the Christian church has allied itself with the ruling powers and consequently with the oppressors. In response, freedom aligned itself with atheism.

In this standoff both the Christian faith and freedom are destroyed. Therefore, we Christians must do everything we can to overcome this false alternative. We can overcome it only when we become radical again and seriously consider who it is in whom we actually believe and what our authentic experience of God is. For that we must rediscover the long-forgotten subversive traditions of freedom in the Bible.

The "God of Abraham, Isaac, and Jacob" is not the God of the pharaohs, the caesars, and the slaveholders. That God is the God who led the Hebrew people out of slavery into freedom. The First Commandment begins: "I am the Lord your God, who brought you out of the land of Egypt, out of the house of bondage [Exod. 20:2]." All other commandments of God are based on this fact. This is the Old Testament definition of God: God the liberator. The experience of God is therefore the experience of the exodus. To believe in God means nothing less than to experience one's own liberation. The people of Israel, who came forth out of slavery, could speak of God's power and of their freedom in one breath. In every Passover festival they celebrate anew how God led them out of slavery into freedom. The modern alternative, God or freedom, sounds absurd here. The opposite is true. The name "God" means freedom. The experience of God—this is our real liberation.

Neither is the "God of our Lord Jesus Christ," of whom the New Testament speaks, the God of rulers and slaveholders. This God is rather the one who raised Jesus from the dead and brought him into the splendor of the divine kingdom. This God is called "God" because of these deeds. This is the God of the humiliated, abandoned, battered Jesus, crucified by the Roman occupational forces in the name of the Roman Empire and the Roman gods. Whoever believes in Jesus and follows him abandons the gods of power and of success, those demon idols of oppression and humiliation.

Who is the real and true God? The New Testament says, "God is the one who raised Jesus from the dead." This is the New Testament definition of God: God, the liberator from the power of sin and of death. This God's power is life-creating power. Therefore the experience of God is the experience of resurrection. To believe in this God means nothing less than leaving behind resignation and oppression and reaching out for freedom. To believe in this God means to stand up and be free. The people of Christ, who remember the crucified Christ in the eucharist and who hope in the messianic future of Christ, therein experience their unending freedom. "Where the Spirit of the Lord is, there is freedom [2 Cor. 3:17]." The modern alternative, God *or* freedom, sounds absurd to Christians as well. The opposite is true: God means freedom from sin and death. The experience of God is our unending freedom.

At the heart of the Old Testament traditions is the exodus from political slavery into the promised land. At the heart of the New Testament traditions is resurrection from death into the life of the messianic kingdom. Why aren't the exodus and the resurrection at the heart of all church traditions in Christianity? Why is the divine majesty portrayed and honored in the churches more analogous to the majesty of earthly rulers than to the picture of the crucified Christ and the resurrected Liberator of the poor? Christians and churches must learn to reorder their thinking if they want to spread the spirit of freedom.

How do we relate exodus theology and resurrection theology to each other? Exodus theology is not yet resurrection theology, but resurrection theology must always include exodus theology and must again and again be embodied in acts that liberate the oppressed.[5]

There is one simple but often overlooked question that neither liberation theology nor resurrection theology must suppress: Who pays the price of freedom? According to the exodus story, Pharaoh and his army must be destroyed that Israel may become free. This negative side of liberation belongs inevitably to the root experience of Israel, the destruction of the demonic power. When prophets subsequently promised the people in the Babylonian Exile the new and final exodus into freedom, they developed various concepts about the "ransom" for Israel. Is it faraway peoples who will be sacrificed (see Isaiah 43:3-4)? Is it the people of Babylon who have to pay the price? The apocalyptic writers knew about the exodus struggle, exaggerating it into universal and cosmic dimensions. It is the "last battle" of God against all God's enemies. Out of the pharaoh of history they made the Antichrist; out of the historical Babylon they made the great whore; out of the chaos at the beginning of creation they made the beast out of the bottomless pit. When the exodus motif became a religious-political motif in the European and North American revolutionary history, especially since the Puritan revolution, there was spread along with the liberation of the oppressed the friend-foe apocalypticism, the idea of total warfare, psychological warfare, and the "last battle": the Armageddon nightmare.[6]

There is, however, in the Old Testament prophecy another answer to the question of the sacrifice or ransom. This other answer can be found in the servant-of-God hymns of Second Isaiah: God sends a servant to pay the ransom for Israel's liberation, to pay the price of freedom. God takes on the necessary burden and the sacrifices of the liberation of humankind. It follows that Israel's freedom has its deepest root in God's own suffering.

This is very important, because only on the grounds of this experience of God is true liberation different from a struggle for existence in which it is the fittest that always survive. The God of the exodus is a God of power, the God of the oppressed. The liberated people therefore sang and sing it again, "I will sing to the Lord, for he has triumphed gloriously; the horse and his rider he has thrown into the sea [Exod. 15:1]," and the old and the new Miriams will take timbrels in their hands and dance and sing (Exodus 15:20-21). But is not Egypt also God's beloved child? Did God not suffer and cry when Egypt was sacrificed for Israel's liberation?

An old Jewish legend in the Babylonian Talmud expressed this in a moving way: "In that very hour when the Egyptians were drowned in the sea, the angels wanted to praise God with a hymn. God, however, praised be the holy name, shouted, 'Human beings created by me are dying in the sea, and you want to rejoice?' "[7]

"The servant of God," however, shows another power. He liberates by taking the suffering on himself: "Upon him was the chastisement that made us whole, and with his stripes we are healed [Isa. 53:5]." Freedom born out of suffering is no privilege and is not exclusive. Israel's freedom born out of God's suffering will bring freedom to the nations but not demand sacrifices.

In the New Testament one can see that God's power is revealed not only in the glorious resurrection of Christ but also in the offering of Christ to death on the cross. Resurrection freedom is an inclusive freedom, because the price, the ransom, of liberation is paid already in the suffering and death of Christ. A truly Christian liberation theology is therefore at its core a theology of the cross: God became human that human beings should gain divine freedom. God is humiliated that human beings may stand up. God suffers death, that humans may live.[8] Let all people therefore recognize that the ground of our freedom is the cross of Christ, the power of our freedom is the resurrection of Christ, and the truth of our freedom is life-giving, creative love.

LIBERATED FAITH

Faith is too often misunderstood as only a formal affirmation of the teaching of the church, yes, often even a blind obedience to ecclesiastical commandments. But liberated faith is faith that grasps people personally. The only truth that makes people free is the truth they affirm because they understand it, not because they are forced to affirm it.

This personal faith is the beginning of a freedom that renews the individual life and, as it says in the Bible, "overcomes the world" (see 1 John 5:4). This faith is an experience that never leaves once it has occurred—the liberation from anxiety to trust, the rebirth into a living hope, the grasping of love that fills us completely. "For freedom Christ has set us free," the apostle Paul said. "Stand fast therefore, and do not submit again to a yoke of slavery [Gal. 5:1]." Through faith one is not freed simply from one form of domination to another, as has often happened in political history. Through faith one is freed to freedom. Wherever we are grasped by the true faith, there we experience our own resurrection into the true life even before death. There we breathe the free air of an incomparable hope. There we rise up out of our defeat and no longer lie conquered on the ground. "Look up and raise your head [Luke 21:28]," it says in the Bible. We learn the steady step and walk upright.

Which freedom do we speak about in this context of Christian faith? The Greeks and the Chinese understood freedom as the integration of the individual into the polis and as the integration of the polis into a cosmic order determined by divine reason and divine law. Whoever conforms to the divine in the cosmos is truly free. For the Greeks, freedom was insight into necessity. What kind of necessity? Divine necessity.

In the modern world many understand freedom as the independent control of individuals over their own lives and possessions, and as the sovereign control of political bodies, peoples, or states over themselves and their possessions. Today freedom is understood as lordship or domination.

For the Christian faith, however, freedom does not mean "insight into necessity," as it did for the Greeks. Nor does freedom mean the independent and sovereign control of one's self and one's possessions. If Christian faith is trust in the God of the exodus, the God of the resurrected Christ, then through faith we participate in this power of liberation and resurrection. Through faith we participate in nothing more and nothing less than the creative power of God. "With God all things are possible," says one Gospel (Matthew 19:26). Who can contradict that? "All things are possible to those who believe," says another Gospel (Mark 9:23). God reveals inexhaustible and abundant possibilities in the creative act of the resurrection of the dead Christ. Whoever trusts in this God participates

61

through the Spirit in God's inexhaustible creative possibilities. Resurrected faith leads to a new, creative life precisely where death reigns and the people have been conquered and have given up all hope. Faith awakens trust in the abundance of divine possibilities. Faith means, therefore, to cross over the boundaries of given reality and to live in the project of hope. Freedom in faith is participation in God's eternal life.

Christianity won the ancient world with the message of this freedom: "All things are yours, whether . . . the world or life or death or the present or future, all are yours; and you are Christ's; and Christ is God's [1 Cor. 3:21-22]." Christ came to break through the boundaries of our limitations. Death, this utmost limitation of humankind, even death itself is defeated. Where have we ever heard of such a freedom? The history of freedom began in our world with this message of freedom. And freedom is the meaning of each individual life history and of our entire world history.[9] Liberation is therefore the experience and the abiding task of true, authentic Christianity.

WHICH FREEDOM DO WE SEEK: LORDSHIP OR FELLOWSHIP?

Politicians and revolutionaries, pietists and atheists—many people talk about freedom, but they do not mean the same thing. Obviously, it is not easy to define freedom. There are so many freedoms: freedom of religion, freedom of conscience, freedom of thought, freedom of trade, free economic exchange, free enterprise, free love, and even alcohol-free drinks. There are many things we call free. What then do we mean by freedom? And what is true freedom?

The first definition we know from political history defines freedom as lordship. Since all previous history can be interpreted as a continuing battle for power, the so-called free, the victors in battle, are those who rule. Those who lose, who are subjected and exploited, are called unfree. The linguistic history of the word freedom itself demonstrates its heritage in a slave society. In such a society only the lord was free; the slaves, the wives, the children over whom he ruled were not free. They were possessions, sealed and sanctioned by the tenth commandment, which forbade the men, of course, to lust after their neighbor's possessions—a man, wife, ox, ass, whatever he possessed. The apostle Paul also uses this language when he speaks about these conflicts, which are overcome in the Christian community: Jew and heathen, man and woman, free and slave.

But those who understand freedom as lordship can be free only at the expense of others. This freedom means oppression for others; one person's richness makes others poor, one person's power oppresses slaves, women, and children. For that reason rulers, ruling classes, and dominating nations always have security problems with their freedom.

Those who understand freedom as lordship really know only themselves and their possessions, and know themselves not as people but as proprietors. They do not know other people as persons, but only as those who "have" and those who "have not."

C.B. Macpherson has made this clear in his important book *The Political Theory of Possessive Individualism* (1962). The results of his historical analysis of the concept of freedom in the beginning of the modern world can be summarized as follows:

- Freedom is a function of property.
- Society consists of the exchange relationships of proprietors.
- Each person is an individual, because he or she is no longer defined by social relationships (family, clan, tribe, nation, humankind), but by property relationships.
- What makes a human being human is freedom, and freedom is ownership of one's self and one's property.

This is still the possessive individualism of modern society.[10]

When we say today that people who can do or have what they want are free, then we understand freedom as lordship, a lordship of people over themselves. When we say today that someone who is not pressured by inner or outer forces is free, then we understand freedom as lordship. Everyone should be his or her own ruler, his or her own lord, his or her own slaveholder. The fact that the understanding of freedom as lordship comes also out of the male-oriented society is demonstrated already by the inclusive use of the word "lord-ship." There has never been talk of "ladyship." Thus, it is comical even to carry this word over to women: in this sense of freedom the woman becomes her own lord. No man was ever expected to be his own lady.

63

Modern liberalism involves possessive individualism. It replaced royal absolutism and feudalism in Western Europe and remained cast in the mold of the feudal lord. The liberals say that everyone who carries the human face has the same right of freedom. The limit of the freedom of each individual is only the freedom and property of the other. Those who claim their own freedom must respect the same freedom for others. But that means also that for modern liberalism freedom is defined as lordship. Each one sees the other as a competitor in the battle for power and ownership. Each one exists for the other only as the limitation of freedom. Each one is for himself or herself free, but no one takes interest in the other. This results in a society of freer, but lonelier, people. No one cares for the other; everyone cares for himself or herself. Freedom has then really become public. Every person has a right to freedom. But is this really true freedom? Is this not the narcissism of the modern Western world?[11]

The other definition we know from social history defines freedom not as lordship but as community. In my earlier comments on the glory and misery of modern liberalism, I said that the truth of freedom is love. Only in love does human freedom come to its truth. I am free and feel myself to be free when I am recognized and accepted by others and when I, for my part, recognize and accept others. I become truly free when I open my life for others and share it with them, and when others open their lives for me and share their lives with me. Then the other person is no longer a limitation of my freedom but the completion of it. A communal and mutual freedom—that is, our freedom—evolves out of your freedom and my own freedom. In this mutual participation in life, individuals are freed from the limitations of their own individuality. They can transcend themselves in the open community. This is the social side of freedom. We call it love or solidarity. We experience this in the unity of separated individuals. The realization of freedom happens not in "free enterprise," but in "mutual help." In mutual help we open ourselves for one another and thus liberate ourselves. In mutual help the powerless become strong again and will survive.[12]

Divide et impera—divide and conquer—this is and was the well-known method of lordship. As long as freedom means lordship, people must separate, isolate, segregate, and differentiate everything in order to control it. But if freedom means community, then one experiences the wholeness of all separated things. The isolation of person from person, the separation of human society from nature, the cleavage of soul and body, and finally the estrangement of human beings from God will each be put aside. People experience true liberation when they once again become one with the other and with nature and with God. Freedom as community thus runs counter to the history of power and class struggles, where freedom is seen only as lordship. In freedom as community, it is no longer only possessions with which one does what one will. The oppressed and the handicapped, women and children, will be taken seriously in their human dignity. Their human rights will be restored and, if necessary, fought for. Nature will no longer be subjected to blind exploitation. It will be respected as the home of humankind. Those whose bodies are seen only as worldly possessions will experience a new existence as they are. The body will no longer be a possession, like a car or television set, but an existence. The body is not something I have but who I am. As the English language puts it so beautifully: I am somebody.

The history of German and Anglo-Saxon languages confirms that community is the root of the word freedom: Whoever is free is friendly, well disposed, open, delightful, and loving. This understanding is found in the concept of hospitality—in the German *gastfrei*, which means, literally, "free for guests." Those who are hospitable never rule over their guests and they are never without them. They are capable of community with strangers. They let strangers participate in their life; they are interested in the lives of others.

Freedom as lordship destroys community. Freedom as lordship is freedom in its untruth. The truth of human freedom lies in love. It leads to unrestricted, solid, and open communities of mutual help. Only this freedom as community can heal the wounds, which freedom as lordship has caused and continues to cause.

FREEDOM AS RESURRECTION

The definition of freedom in the Christian faith goes beyond freedom as community. We have characterized faith for the Christian as essentially resurrection hope. Freedom in light of this hope is the creative passion for the possible. It is not, as in lordship, directed

65

only to the things at hand. It is set up not only as love for the community of people at hand but also directed toward the future, the future of the coming God. The future of God is the limitless treasure of possibilities, while the past represents the limited kingdom of reality. Creative passion is always directed toward the project of such a future. We will implement new, as yet unthought-of possibilities. Thus, we strain with passion toward the future, and in this yearning our reason is transformed into productive imagination. We dream the messianic dream of a new, whole, totally lived life. We explore the possibilities of the future in order to fulfill this dream of life. This future dimension of freedom has been overlooked for a long time, because the freedom of Christian faith as participation in the ongoing creative work of God has been so long misunderstood and because, previously, religious anxiety rather than messianic hope ruled even Christianity. In truth, freedom in faith is expectant creativity.

Earlier I spoke of freedom either as lordship in the relationship of subject and object, or as community in the relationship of subject and subject. Freedom, however, is the orientation of both subjects toward a common project. Without this dimension of project, freedom is not yet fully understood. In the orientation to a common project, freedom is creative movement. Whoever transcends the present, whoever enters the future in thought and word and deed, is truly free.

Let me give some examples. The United States of America is one great project of modern humanity. People from all nations, races, classes, and traditions came to North America and formed a new community as it never happened before in the history of humankind. The visions of freedom, of human rights, and of the self-government of the people formed this project. "America" was the dream of oppressed people in Europe, and their visions and hopes became "the American dream."[13] As far as I understand this project, it still seems to be unfinished: You can succeed, you can fail—the future is in your hands.

The Soviet Union is another great project of modern humanity. The "first socialist country" understands itself as the homeland of the proletariat in all nations and the great friend of all oppressed nations. The visions of justice and equality, of socialism and solidarity, for everyone on earth formed this Russian project. Socialism was the other dream of the oppressed people in Europe.[14] As far as I understand this Soviet project, it seems to be another unfinished project, full of disappointments and perversion, but not without hope.

As a poor Old European, full of humility between those two mountains of power and arrogance, I still have the dream of peace and share the following project: no democracy without socialism and no socialism without democracy. I therefore work for more economic justice in the West and for more freedom and human rights in the East. I want to see a covenant between personal freedom and social security, between economic justice and political responsibility, for everyone. And I still believe that this vision is a real possibility, although I experience disappointments and defeats. But disappointment is never the refutation of hope; it is an experience only hope makes possible.

From the perspective of hope there is yet another dimension of freedom. Freedom is not a possession; freedom is an event. We experience freedom in the events of liberation and of creativity. We experience freedom in the history of our liberations. We are never already free. We can become, but we are not yet, permanently free. What we call freedom is the result of real liberation. The reality of freedom itself is given first in the perfected realm of freedom. Here in the history of sin and death and evil powers we experience events, processes, and occurrences of liberation. Let us use a biblical analogy. Here in history we have freedom only in the ongoing "exodus" from slavery and in the long march through the desert; we seek the promised land. Therefore freedom is the goal of all liberation, not its abstract presupposition. It is better, because it is more realistic to search for liberation than it is to praise and to idealize one's freedom.

It follows from this that in history freedom came always and only in struggle. Historical freedom has two sides. It is living in the category of the "nevertheless" and in the category of the "how much more," as Paul Ricoeur so strikingly clarified it with reference to my *Theology of Hope*.[15] Historical freedom comes from resistance and hope.

Against what does freedom exercise its resistance? Christian faith, as we said, is at the heart resurrection faith. Thus it opposes death with a passion. Hope loves life, not death. Not until life is fully snatched away from death is it fully lived. Hope cannot be content with anything less.

67

But which death is meant here? Death is not only the natural end of a human life. Death is also a personal, social, and political power in the midst of life. Threats of death are terrifying. Anxiety about death suppresses and exploits. The handicapped, the old, and the sick in our society are threatened with social death when the healthy break off all relationships with them. Finally, there are many people who have surrendered themselves to a spiritual death, and have become feelingless and apathetic. They do not care about anything. They are stiffened like corpses, even though they are still in the midst of their lives. Death has many faces. Freedom in the perspective of hope sets itself over against anxiety and apathy, over against the loud death of bombs and the creeping death of souls. There are so many forms of death and dying that need not be. Whoever loves life, whoever hopes in the resurrection, has the power to overcome the faces of death.

To what does freedom direct its hope? "For how much more" says the apostle Paul so often when he speaks no longer of "freedom from" but of "freedom to." How much greater is the future than the past! How much greater is God's grace than the sins of humankind! How much greater is the freedom in the free world than the freedom from slavery! Indeed, we learn from historical experience that the negative from which we seek freedom is far easier to express than the positive which we hope to become. But it is the hope in the greater future that leads us in history to ever-new experiences. That is the "how much more" of hope in life. That is the surplus value of the future in history.

That "nevertheless," with which the hope of the oppressed resists suffering and death, belongs together with a surplus of confidence. If it is not to be mere blatant reaction, the necessary resistance must be based in hope. And if it is not to be mere illusion, hope must lead us to the necessary resistance against death and against those who spread death.

THE CRY FROM THE DEPTHS

I have told you about freedom. I have talked about the liberating God who led people out of slavery into historical freedom and Jesus out of death into eternal freedom. I have described true Christian faith as the experience of the great liberation to new creative life. And I have placed three ideas of freedom over against one another: freedom as lordship, freedom as community, and freedom as expectant creativity. In doing this, I have tried to argue that the modern European alternative "God or freedom" is false. No doubt Christians and churches themselves are guilty, whenever they have fought in the name of religion against the freedom of humanity, whenever they have identified themselves with powers of oppression. Nevertheless, the true Christian faith is again and again an encompassing experience of freedom: God is our unending freedom! Freedom has not been well preserved in atheism. It is faith in the resurrection that gives us true courage for freedom.

Whoever wishes to speak of freedom must begin with liberation, but whoever wants liberation must first hear the cry from the depths to our ears and to our hearts. The key to our own freedom lies with the enslaved. As long as they cannot become free, we too are never really free. As long as we do not live in an open community with them, we are captives ourselves. This is the modern ideology of national security for which we are foolish enough to sacrifice even our social security. There is a growing and politically exploited fear of the loss of our freedom which repressed our older hope of winning our freedom. Many wealthy nations today are preparing themselves psychologically and militarily to secure their freedom. The best safeguard of freedom, however, is the liberation of people who suffer under our domination and our indifference and who hope for our solidarity.

> Du, edle Freiheit, Du,
> Wer sich nicht dir ergibt,
> Der weiss nicht was ein Mensch,
> Der Freiheit liebt, liebt.

> You, Noble Freedom,
> Whoever is not committed to you
> Will never know what the one,
> Who loves freedom, loves.

Angelus Silesius said it, and I think we can agree: "Wer Freiheit liebt, liebt Gott" (Whoever loves freedom loves God).

5

The Trinitarian
Story of Jesus

I want to tell a story, the story of Jesus our brother, the God story of Jesus, Jesus' story with the God whom he called so intimately "Abba," dear father, and God's story with him, as beloved son. We shall discover that this God story of Jesus is a trinitarian story, the love story between the Son and the Father and the Holy Spirit. The doctrine of the Trinity is not a speculation over mysteries in heaven, which nobody knows; it is rather the short formulation of the God story of Jesus, the son of the Abba-father in heaven and our brother on earth.[1]

The doctrine of the Trinity enjoys no particular popularity in Western Christianity. It is true that the Christian liturgy traditionally begins with the trinitarian invocation "In the name of the Father and of the Son and of the Holy Spirit," but it is also true that many Christians, including many theologians, find it difficult to speak about God at all. In an atheistic world tortured with the questions "Does God exist?" or "Is God dead?" they have simply forgotten the doctrine of the Trinity. Modern Christian belief in God is at best Christian monotheism. What is beyond that appears only

70

as speculation about mysteries we are unable to understand.

Is there any witness to the Trinity in the New Testament? Modern liberal Protestantism has denied that there is. It has said that the doctrine of the Trinity develops only later in the process called the Hellenization of Christianity. Assimilation of Neoplatonic speculation forced the theologians of the ancient church into trinitarian thinking in their philosophical concepts of God. And with this, the simple and human message of Jesus was replaced with a speculative dogma describing the relationship between the persons of God the Father and the eternal Son and the Holy Spirit. Against the influence of Hellenization, Adolf von Harnack asserted, "The Father alone, and not the Son, is the message of the gospel, as Jesus himself proclaimed it."[2] He challenged the church to return to "the simple gospel of Jesus." But is von Harnack's view of the Trinity really true? Is the confession of divine sonship of Jesus only a later apotheosis, a herocult dreamed up by frustrated disciples?

I shall tell the God story of Jesus in four stages and will show the changing trinitarian structures in each. For this we must look at Jesus "from below" and "from above," from a pre-Easter perspective and from a post-Easter perspective, in order to recognize him in the wholeness of his relationships. The four stages are:

1. The baptism of Jesus and the sending of the Son
2. The passion of Jesus and the delivering up of the Son
3. The resurrection of Jesus and the revelation of the Son
4. The parousia of Jesus and the return of the Son to the Father

At the end we shall ask for the theological consequences of our survey (1) for the biblical understanding of the Triune God, (2) for the social understanding of the unity of the Triune God, and (3) for a new concept of God as "the motherly Father."

1. THE BAPTISM OF JESUS AND THE SENDING OF THE SON

We begin with the story of Jesus as it is presented in the synoptic Gospels. One fact is well documented: Before the official appearance

Hildegard of Bingen, The Trinity

of Jesus, John the Baptizer appeared in the area of the Jordan, calling the people of Israel to repentance. Another fact is well documented: Jesus of Nazareth was one of the disciples of John.[3]

Jesus believed in the divine commission of the Baptizer and said that John's baptism was "from God [Mark 11:30]"; he "came to you in the way of righteousness [Matt. 21:32]" and there was "no one greater [Matt. 11:11]," said Jesus. Jesus was probably baptized with the repentant crowds (Luke 3:7). But with this particular baptism something unusual happened to Jesus. All reports witness to it: "The Spirit of God descended upon him." This signified Jesus' calling to be a prophet, an *ish-ha-ruach*, a Spirit-filled person, a Spirit-bearer. But it also signified the eschatological return of the Holy Spirit, which had been extinguished in Israel since the time of the prophets, and this in turn signified nothing less than the beginning of the messianic age, when the Spirit "would be poured out on all flesh [Joel 2:28]."

The messianic importance of the baptism of Jesus with the Spirit is portrayed in the vision of a heaven opening up and in the sound of a heavenly voice. According to the reports, a divine proclamation followed the descent of the Spirit: "This is my beloved Son, with whom I am well pleased [Matt. 3:17]." But who is this Son? The customary allusion is to the royal psalm, Psalm 2:7: "I will tell of the decree of the Lord: He said to me, 'You are my son, today I have begotten you.' " If that is correct, then Jesus through his baptism was established as the messianic king of Israel.

This is grounded in the fact that the baptism experience of Jesus apparently refers to a special revelation that Matthew reports: "All things have been delivered to me by my Father; and no one knows the Son except the Father, and no one knows the Father except the Son and any one to whom the Son chooses to reveal him [Matt. 11:27]." The words are somewhat enigmatic, but there is nothing to contest their authenticity. These words of revelation show exactly what distinguished Jesus from John the Baptist; they point to the reason that Jesus had to separate himself from John.

John proclaimed the coming kingdom as the judgment of God: "Even now the axe is laid to the root of the trees; every tree therefore that does not bear good fruit is cut down and thrown into the fire [Matt. 3:10]." But Jesus proclaimed the coming kingdom as the grace of God, because the Lord of this kingdom was his Father.

The content of the revelation that fell to Jesus' lot through his baptism and calling lies in this name of God: "Abba, Father."[4] The revelation of the name Father is the new and unique herald of the coming kingdom. According to the Gospels, Jesus never addressed God as "Our Father" or even as "Father" in general, but always and exclusively as "my Father in heaven." He always proclaimed "my Father in heaven." From this it follows that Jesus must have understood his relationship to God as that of the Son to the Father. More particularly, it follows that he must have understood himself in relation to God as "Son," indeed as "the Son," if not even as "the only" and "own" Son of God.[5] As the Son, he revealed the Father. In community with the Father, his own relationship with God is experienced by others in faith. We must finally reject Harnack's judgment: not the Father alone, but the Son with the Father is the message of the gospel, and this is not only the message of the apostolic Gospels, it is already the gospel of Jesus himself.

In the synoptic Gospels, Jesus' proclamation begins with his baptism in the Spirit and the calling revealed in it. For this reason it is understandable that Paul, from a post-Easter perspective, saw the historical calling of Jesus as his eternal sending from the Father. The sending formula is always connected with the name of the Son, and it always refers to the liberation of men and women to a new and intimate relationship with the Abba-Father of Jesus in heaven.[6] "But when the time had fully come, God sent forth the Son, born of woman, born under the law, to redeem those who were under the law, so that we might receive adoption as heirs" (see Galatians 4:4). The sending of the Son here includes the birth and circumcision of Jesus, for it is directed to the deliverance of those enslaved under the law and points to freedom of the children of God, the *hypothesia*. The Father is the sender, sending the Son to draw believers into a relationship of child and parent. The Son was subjected to the law to redeem those under the law and to bring them into his own life with the Father. Romans 8:3 is another sending formula: sending God's "own Son in the likeness of sinful flesh and for sin, [God] condemned sin in the flesh, in order that the just requirement of the law might be fulfilled in us, who walk not according to the flesh but according to the Spirit." Again the Father is the sender, and the one sent is depicted powerfully as God's "own Son" (see Romans 8:32). The purpose of the sending itself is life in the Spirit. It is

74

much the same in Romans 8:15: "For you did not receive the spirit of slavery to fall back into fear, but you have received the spirit of sonship. When we cry, 'Abba! Father!' it is the Spirit bearing witness." When Paul here inserts the Semitic word *abba* into his Greek text, he is certainly following the proclamation and prayer of the historical Jesus himself.

At this first station of the God story of Jesus we meet the first biblical structure of the Trinity.

- The Father sends the Son through the Holy Spirit.
- The Son comes from love of the Father and in the power of the Spirit.
- The Son comes to bring people into his own intimate community with God his Abba-Father and to fill them with the liberating power of the Spirit.

2. The Passion of Jesus and the Delivering Up of the Son

The passion history of Jesus has an outer and an inner dimension. In its outer dimension it is the story of Jesus' rejection by his own people as a blasphemer of God and of his execution by the Romans as an agitator against the Roman government. In its inner dimension it is the story of Jesus' abandonment by the God he called "my Father" and whose kingdom he had proclaimed to the poor. The stories of Gethsemane and Golgotha tell of this inner dimension of the passion of Jesus.

In the night before his betrayal, Jesus took three of his disciples and went into the Garden of Gethsemane. There, as Mark writes, he "began to be greatly distressed and troubled. . . . 'My soul is very sorrowful, even to death' [Mark 14:33-34]." And he asked his friends to stay and watch with him. So many nights in the past he had withdrawn from the disciples to unite himself with his Father in the prayer of the heart. But that night in Gethsemane, for the first time, he cannot bear to be alone with his Abba-God. He obviously fears God and seeks the protection of his friends. Then comes the prayer that in its original form sounds more like a challenge:

75

"Abba, Father, all things are possible to thee; remove this cup from me [Mark 14:36]." That is, spare me this suffering.

The real passion of Christ begins with this prayer that was not answered, with this dread of abandonment by the God he called "Father." For the Son the terrifying silence of the Father in response to his prayer in Gethsemane is deeper than the silence of death. Martin Buber called this "the eclipse of God." It is expressed by the mystics as "the dark night of the soul": The Father withdraws. And God is silent. This is the experience of hell. Martin Luther based his doctrine of Christ's "descent into hell" on this agony of Jesus in Gethsemane. He pictured this quite powerfully: "Not only in the eyes of the world and the disciples, but even in his own eyes, Christ saw himself abandoned and forsaken by God. In his own consciousness he felt himself execrated by God, cast into the torment of the damned, forever to experience the eternal wrath of God, forever to be frightened and fleeing before it." For Luther the real passion of Christ was the passion of Christ abandoned by God. Christ was far from the perfect person or the superstar. He was the most vulnerable and the poorest of all "the wretched of this earth." And he was vulnerable to pain and anxiety not only in his human nature, as the scholastic tradition had taught, but in his very person, in his relationship to the Father, that is, in his divine sonship.[7]

At the end of the passion of Christ there is another prayer, the cry with which he died on Golgotha: "My God, my God, why hast thou forsaken me? [Mark 15:34]." For three hours he hung on the cross, waiting in apparent silence for his mortal wounds to carry him into death. Then he died with a cry that betrayed his sense of profound abandonment by the God whom he had called "Abba," the God on whose messianic kingdom he had set his entire life, the God whose son he had thought himself to be.

This must be the historical hard kernel of the Golgotha story, for the idea that the last words of the Savior to God could have been this cry of despair would never have struck into the heart of Christianity had it not been spoken out, had it not been heard in the cry of the dying Christ. What Christ had dreaded, what he had struggled with in Gethsemane, what he had begged the Father to take away from him, is not removed but comes to pass on the cross. The Father has forsaken him, and in this act thrown him into the dread of hell.

He who had known himself to be the Son was abandoned, rejected, and humiliated.

In his theology of delivering up, Paul comes closest to the mystery of Golgotha.[8] In the Gospels, where the death of Jesus is represented in view of his teaching, his life, and his preaching, the Greek word *paradidonai* has a clearly negative connotation. It means delivered up and cast off, betrayed, and repudiated. Paul too, in Romans 1:24, uses the expression "delivered up" (*paredoken*) to depict the wrath and judgment of God over the sins of humankind. Those who have forsaken the invisible God and worshiped the creation instead are forsaken by God and "delivered up" to their mortal greed.

But Paul radically revises the meaning of being "delivered up" when he looks at the abandonment of Jesus on the cross. He explains this abandonment not in view of the life of Jesus but in view of his resurrection. The God who raised Jesus from the dead is the same God who delivered Jesus up to death on the cross. It is in the abandonment on the cross, out of which Jesus cried in anguish "Why?" that Paul finds the answer to Jesus' question. "He who did not spare his own Son but gave him up for us all (*paredoken*), will he not also give us all things with him? [Rom. 8:32]." For this reason the Father abandoned and delivered up his "own Son," as Paul emphasizes here. Elsewhere Paul puts this even more starkly: "Christ redeemed us from the curse of the law, having become a curse for us [Gal. 3:13]." The Father abandoned the Son; he did it "for us," that is, in order to become the Father of all the abandoned. The Son is delivered up in order to become the brother of the accursed and the deliverer of the condemned. According to Galatians 2:20, the Son was not only passively delivered up by the Father. He actively delivered himself up for us. In the action of delivering up, he is not only an object but also the subject. His suffering to death was active passion, a *passio activa*, in which he consciously chose the path of suffering, consenting to death. This is in accord with the Synoptics' representation of the history of the passion of Jesus.

The passion of Jesus signifies, at first, an inner conformity of will between the Son, who was delivered up, and the Father, who delivered him up. This profound conformity of will is also the content of the Gethsemane event, and it is established precisely at the point of widest separation between Father and Son. At the foot of the cross, the Son and the Father are united in a single act of submission.

The letter to the Hebrews expresses this, saying that Christ offered himself as a sacrifice to God "through the eternal Spirit [Heb. 9:14]." The delivering up and the sacrificing of the Son both occur "through the Spirit." The Spirit is the binding force that locks the union and the separation of the Father and the Son together.

Finally, the Gospel of John summarizes this delivering up in the words "For God so loved the world that he gave his only Son, that whoever believes in him should not perish but have eternal life [John 3:16]." To say that God "so" loved the world is to say that God loved the world "in this way," a way that pointed to the Son's death on the cross "for us." Thus 1 John defines God: "God is love [1 John 4:16]." God not only loves, as if God could be angry too. God *is* love. God's very existence is love. God establishes the divine self as love. This is what happens on the cross and what is revealed in the resurrection of Jesus.

A Trinity seen in the light of the cross is a cruciform Trinity and has the following structure:

- The Father delivers up the Son for us.
- The Son delivers himself up for us.
- The Spirit is the medium through which the common sacrifice of the Son and the Father occurs; the Spirit united the abandoned Son with his Father.

In medieval art the Trinity is depicted with the Father on the throne of glory, raising up the cross beam on which the Son hangs. The Holy Spirit is in the form of a dove descending from the face of the Father onto the crucified Son. This is the so-called *Gnaden-stuhl*, the seat of grace.

3. The Resurrection of Jesus and the Revelation of the Son

Jesus was publicly crucified, but the resurrected Lord was seen by only a few women at the grave and by other disciples. Crowds saw his death in weakness and disgrace, but only a few saw his appear-

The "Seat of Grace"

ance in glory. What did the Easter witnesses see? How did they see the Risen One? How did they recognize him?

The Easter vision. To answer these questions we must talk about the Easter vision, the "seeing." The Greek word for "to see" is rich with meaning: *opthe* means Christ "was seen" or Christ "appeared" or Christ "let himself be seen" or God "revealed" him. But each meaning is a formula of revelation, and each formula means to see something that is given in an extraordinary way to someone to be seen.[9]

How then is this Easter "seeing" to be understood? "In the last days" the God of promise will appear in glory and fulfill the hopes of the people and everybody will see him face-to-face, say the prophets of the Old Testament. This text is the context of the resurrection experience. If the resurrected Christ "appeared" to the Easter witnesses, then the appearance must mean the pre-vision, the dawning, of his future in the glory of God. The Easter "seeing" of Christ thus has the structure of the anticipation for his divine future. Whoever sees the resurrected Christ sees into the hidden future of the coming glory of God.

How did Jesus appear? Paul, the last eyewitness to the resurrected Christ, describes it: God "was pleased to reveal the Son to me, in order that I might preach him among the Gentiles [Gal. 1:16]." The resurrected Christ appeared to Paul as the Son. God revealed Jesus to Paul as God's Son. Still filled with this revelation, Paul summed up the power and content of the gospel: Jesus is the Son of God (Romans 1:4,9; 1 Corinthians 1:9; 2 Corinthians 1:19). His mission to the world is the mission of the Son. The "Christian religion" that Paul brought into being through his apocalyptic mission is the messianic religion, the religion of hope, because it is the religion of Jesus the son, the firstborn among many sisters and brothers.

And how did the Father, who had delivered the Son up to death and damnation, raise him up? The biblical witness is clear: through the creative Spirit (Romans 8:11; 1 Timothy 3:16; 1 Peter 3:18), through God's "glory" (Romans 6:4), through God's "power" (1 Corinthians 6:14). "Spirit," "power," and "glory" are consciously used here as synonyms, and they point to something that is neither the

Father nor the Son: they point to the third divine subject in the God story of Jesus, the Spirit.

What aspect of the Trinity is revealed in the resurrection?

- The Father resurrects the Son through the Spirit.
- The Father reveals the Son in the Spirit.
- The Son is established as Lord of the Kingdom through the Spirit of the resurrection.

The sending of the creative Spirit through the Son. Where was Jesus raised up to? Into the heavens? Into the kingdom of God? The answer to these questions is found in understanding the way Jesus was raised from the dead. Jesus is resurrected into the coming glory of God, into the coming kingdom. And Jesus is resurrected into the divine origin of the Spirit. His resurrection signals the sending of the Spirit. God's glory in this world is revealed through Jesus Christ. Christ is the Lord of glory for this segment of trinitarian history, and in his time he is the herald of the time of the life-giving Spirit. Through Christ, the creative Spirit and the energies of the Spirit are poured out on the disciples and the congregations, and through these "onto all flesh."

We are here particularly interested in the relationship between the Son of God and the life-giving Spirit. In the sending, delivering up, and resurrection of Jesus, the Spirit acted on him, and Jesus acted out of the working of the creative Spirit. But now the relationship is reversed. The resurrected Christ sends the Spirit. He is even personally present in the life-giving Spirit, and he works on and with us through the energies of the Spirit, the charismata.

The Spirit witnesses to Christ. Whoever confesses Christ as Lord does so in the power of the Spirit, a power that creates life out of death. For this reason, after Easter the Spirit is called "the spirit of sonship [Rom. 8:15]," "the spirit of faith [2 Cor. 4:13]," and "the Spirit of Christ [Rom. 8:9]." "Where the Spirit of the Lord is, there is freedom [2 Cor. 3:17]."

What aspect of the Trinity do we meet here?

- The Father raises up the dead Son through the life-giving Spirit.

81

- The Father establishes the Son as Lord of the Kingdom.
- The resurrected Son sends the creative Spirit from the Father to renew heaven and earth.
- The Spirit comes from the Father and the Son.

In the history of Jesus until the resurrection, we observed the order: Father—Spirit—Son. We see now in the history of Jesus after the resurrection a different order: Father—Son—Spirit. This means that with the sending of the Spirit, the Trinity is open. In the sending of the creative Spirit, the trinitarian life of God is open to the world, to humanity, and to the future. In the experience of the life-giving Spirit in faith, in baptism, in the congregation, and in worship, we are integrated into the life of the Trinity itself. Through the spirit of Christ we become participants not only in the new creation but also in the eternal trinitarian life of God. To understand why this is true, we are driven to the first biblical mention of the Trinity: baptism.

In the New Testament the explicit triadic formulas are, without exception, baptismal formulas. The theology of the Trinity is indeed the theology of baptism, and it must be, because the New Testament story of the Father, Son, and creative Spirit illustrates the Trinity not as a closed and contained celestial circle but as an open and messianic movement. Through baptism we are drawn into the inner working of this movement. In baptism the doctrine of the Trinity has its *Sitz im Leben*. Baptism is the praxis of the Trinity.

What aspect of the Trinity confronts us in baptism?

- In baptism the divine Trinity is unfolded as the open and eschatological history of God.
- The "unity" of Father, Son, and Spirit is not closed and final, but an open and inviting unity, a community.
- The unity of the triune God is open for unification with the faithful, with humanity, and with the whole of creation.

4. THE PAROUSIA OF JESUS AND THE RETURN OF THE SON TO THE FATHER

In 1 Thessalonians 1:9-10 Paul demands that the people turn away from idols and turn toward the "living and true God." This conversion occurs in the power of the expectation of God's "Son from heaven, whom [God] raised from the dead, Jesus, who delivers us from the wrath to come." The hope of the congregation is here directed to the parousia of Jesus Christ, whom God resurrected from the dead.[10] He will come again as the Son of God, and the expectation of his second coming is the expectation of the Son, our brother. The Son is expected to come as the deliverer of his brothers and sisters through the judgment. Christ appears not as the stern and strange judge but as the trusted and beloved brother. He comes to judge, but one should hope for, not fear, such judgment.

Paul's picture of the eschatological future in 1 Corinthians 15:22-28 is no different from Philippians 2:9-11, only more detailed. He describes the eschatological future as an event in the inner life of the Trinity itself. 1 Corinthians 15:22-28 concerns the future of the history of the world and the fulfillment of divine glory:

> For as in Adam all die, so also in Christ shall all be made alive. But each in his own order: Christ the first fruits, then at his coming those who belong to Christ. Then comes the end, when he delivers the kingdom to God the Father after destroying every rule and every authority and power. For he must reign until he has put all his enemies under his feet. The last enemy to be destroyed is death. . . . When all things are subjected to him, then the Son himself will also be subjected to him who put all things under him, that God may be [all in all].

In the resurrection, the Father gave the divine glory to the Son. In the eschaton, in the fulfillment of all things, the Son returns all glory to the Father. In the end the "kingdom of the Son" becomes "the kingdom of glory" of the triune God, when "God will be all in all." Thus the lordship of Christ has temporal boundaries. It begins in a hidden way with the sending in his baptism and is revealed in his resurrection. The lordship of Christ encompasses both the "living and the dead," and it culminates in the parousia, where Christ quickens the dead and destroys death itself. The ultimate goal of the lordship of Christ is to prepare the way for the kingdom of glory, to prepare for God's indwelling in the new creation; and thus, God will be "all in all."

What structure of the Trinity is recognized in this eschatological future?

- The Father surrenders all things to the Son.
- The Son turns the completed kingdom over to the Father.
- The Son surrenders himself to the Father.

In the fulfillment of salvation and in the glorification of God, the Son is the agent of all action, and the Father is the recipient. In the eschaton, all action proceeds from the Son and the Spirit; the Father receives the kingdom, the power, and the glory in eternity. Which trinitarian order is recognized here?

- In the sending, delivering up, and resurrection of Christ it is Father-Spirit-Son.
- In the lordship of Christ and the sending of the Spirit it is Father-Son-Spirit.
- In the horizon of eschatological fulfillment and glorification it is Spirit-Son-Father.

THEOLOGICAL CONSEQUENCES

The God story of Jesus is the trinitarian story of the Son. The trinitarian story of Jesus is the story of the open, inviting communal relationships of God. In the story of Jesus, the Father, the Son, and the Holy Spirit do not work together in only one pattern. In the sending, the delivering up, and the resurrection of the Son, the Father is the agent of action. The Son is the recipient of the action of the Father, and the Holy Spirit is the medium through which the Father acts and the Son becomes obedient to the Father's will.

In the kingdom of the Son and in the pouring out of the Holy Spirit, the Son, along with the Father, is the agent of action, and the Holy Spirit receives her sending from the Son and takes her point of departure from the Father.

In the end, finally, the Son is the agent of action. He delivers the kingdom over to the Father, and the Holy Spirit is the agent

Andrei Rubljov, Trinity, 1415

Pietà

God the Father with the Corpse of Christ

of action, glorifying the Son and the Father with the joy and the praise of the renewed and transfigured creation. The Father is in the end only recipient; he receives the perfected kingdom from the Son and receives the eternal bliss and glory from the Holy Spirit.

The creation of the world, the reconciliation, and the final redemption of the world is nothing other than the history of the changing communal relationships of the Triune God; it is the great love story of the Father, the Son, and the Holy Spirit, a divine love story in which we all are involved together with heaven and earth.

The unity of the Triune God is divine comm-unity, which is open for us, for the world, and for our future. The trinitarian story of Jesus reveals the trinitarian story of God, and the trinitarian story of God as the eternal divine life of the Triune God. This divine life is revealed through Jesus and the Holy Spirit, and if it is revealed, it is also opened up for us and the whole of creation. Revelation is an invitation, that is, the inauguration of a new situation of God for us. How then is the unity of God to be understood? In the trinitarian story of Jesus, we see the three divine subjects working together. The trinitarian story of Jesus is the common working, the cooperation of the Father, the Son, and the Spirit. If this is true, then the unity of God cannot be a monadic unity. The unity of the Triune God is rather the unique divine community. The unity of the Father with the Son and the Holy Spirit lies in their personal community rather than in a common divine substance or in the identity of one, absolute, divine subjectivity. Remember Jesus' high-priestly prayer (John 17:21ff.) "that they may all be one, even as thou, Father, art in me, and I in thee, that they also may be in us." The community of the disciples and friends of Jesus among one another should conform to the unique unity of the Father and the Son. They should live with one another and even in one another, just as the Father lives in the Son and the Son lives in the Father. Their community not only should reflect the community of the Father and the Son, but could also participate in the divine community of the Son and the Father. This presupposes that the community of the Triune God is so wide open that as humanity and nature are united in love, the entire creation will find space and time in God. The unity of the Triune God is open and inviting for the unification of the entire creation not only with it but also in it.

***Does trinitarian thinking overcome theological patriarchalism? Jesus'
Abba-Father is the motherly Father.*** "No one knows the Son except
the Father, and no one knows the Father except the Son and any
one to whom the Son chooses to reveal him [Matt. 11:27]." This
synoptic word clarifies the Christian understanding of the Fatherhood of God. God the Father is the Father of his Son Jesus. Fatherhood is determined exclusively by his relationship with this Son
Jesus. Only the Son reveals who God the Father is and what the
Fatherhood of God means. Whoever wants to understand God the
Father in a Christian way must therefore forget the patriarchal Father-
religion and focus on the life and the message of Jesus of Nazareth.
"Who has seen me has seen the Father [John 14:9]." It is Jesus,
who reveals the Abba mystery of God to us, and it is in the spirit
of freedom that we enter into the intimacy of his relationship with
God and can also pray, "Abba! Father! [Rom. 8:15]." Freedom in
the Spirit distinguishes the Father of Jesus Christ from the world
patriarch of the Father religion, where there is only subjugation in
the spirit of fear.

If the Son comes from the Father alone, then the coming forth
must be thought of as both "procreation" and "birth." This is a
significant change in the Father concept. A father who both begets
and gives birth to a son is no mere male father but rather is a
motherly father.[11] He cannot be defined as single-sexed, but as
bisexual or transsexual. He is both the motherly father of the only-
begotten Son, and the fatherly mother of the only-born son. According to the old and orthodox Council of Toledo 675, "we must
believe that the Son came from the womb of the Father [*de utero
patris*] and was begotten or born [*genitus vel natus*] from the Father's own being." The motherly Father of Jesus Christ is no longer
the God of patriarchal monotheism. Not a society under male domination, but only a human fellowship free from sexism and class rule
can become the image of the Triune God on earth.

Pantheism ("mother earth") was the religion of the early matriarchal culture. Monotheism ("heavenly Father") was and is the religion
of the patriarchal cultures. The trinitarian understanding of God
points to a messianic future beyond matriarchy and patriarchy, a
future of human fellowship without domination and submission. And
this is the "fellowship of the Holy Spirit [2 Cor. 13:14]," who may
be with us all.

6

The Social Understanding of the Trinity

THE CORRELATION BETWEEN KNOWLEDGE OF GOD AND KNOWLEDGE OF SELF

There is no self-knowledge without the knowledge of God, and no knowledge of God without our self-knowledge. With this thesis Calvin began his *Institutes of the Christian Religion*: "All our wisdom, insofar as it really deserves the name wisdom and is real and dependable, embraces basically two aspects: the knowledge of God and our self-knowledge. These two hang together in various ways, and it is therefore not easy to say which stands in the prior place and produces the other out of itself." Calvin elected to follow the "right order of doctrine" and thus dealt with the knowledge of God first, followed then by the knowledge of self. That the correlation of theology and anthropology is indissoluble is a universal Christian conviction.[1]

But why does human self-knowledge have this special nearness to the knowledge of God? Why not begin, for example, with a knowledge of nature and discover from there a correlation between the knowledge of God and a knowledge of nature? The basis for the

90

exclusive preference for self-knowledge based in the knowledge of God lies in the exceptional position of the human being in nature. Biblically this is described as the image of God.

> Then God said, "Let us make [human beings] in our image, after our likeness. . . ." So God created [human beings] in his own image, in the image of God he created [them]; male and female he created them—Genesis 1:26-27

In nature, humans perceive the works of God; in themselves and others as humans, they perceive the image of God, an image that corresponds to God and represents God in the creation. That is why the knowledge of God which arises from God's own image is a clearer and more certain knowledge than that knowledge which arises from God's works. And that is why human self-knowledge is dependent on a knowledge of God, for how can human beings understand themselves as the image of God if they do not know who God is? How shall people learn to understand God when they do not simultaneously begin to understand themselves as the image of God?

Whatever the "image of God" means in particular instances, in every case that which represents God and corresponds to God, and that in which God recognizes the divine self, is intended. Human beings are the image of God on earth insofar as they correspond to God and represent the invisible God in the visible world. Human beings are the image of God on earth insofar as God recognizes the divine self in them as in a mirror. The works of creation are an expression of the will of God, but God's image on earth must be understood as the expression and reflection of God's nature.

THE CORRELATION BETWEEN MONOTHEISM AND LORDSHIP

The correlation between theology and anthropology can be seen particularly clearly in the history of Christian theology. Here we will follow the development of monotheism and its reception into the Christian concept of God and will examine the corresponding development in the concept of the human.

Monotheism and monarchy. In book 12 of his *Metaphysics*, Aristotle presents his philosophical theology. He concludes his exposition of the One, the Unchangeable, the Divine Being, with a quote from the *Iliad*: "Being, however, did not want to be governed badly; rule by many is not good. Let one be the Lord." The cosmos, according to this, has a monarchical structure: one God, one law, one world. God is the guarantee of the unity of the world. The world is dependent on God, although God is not within it. The many yearn for the One, and the One is the measure of the many. This is the first centralist world theory in our Western tradition.

It is noteworthy that this quotation from the *Iliad* comes from the political realm. Agamemnon united the mutually hostile Greek cities against the Trojans with the cry, "Let one be the Lord." We can see here the clear correspondence between metaphysical theory and political theory. Did Aristotle have the Greek monarchy of Alexander the Great in mind as he formulated his metaphysical views? When the political order can be realized only by virtue of its correspondence to the cosmological order, then the political world will be organized in a similar way: one king, one will, one kingdom.[2] And because metaphysical monotheism is universal, the corresponding political monarchy must become imperial. Otherwise there can be no ordered world in which many peoples are unified in peace under the one God. The political theologies developed in the theocratic empire of Byzantium, and later in the time of European absolutism, by praising the one imperial ruler as the exalted image of the one God, legitimized God's dominion.[3] But this idea is not Christian at all. Genghis Khan (1162-1227) justified his mongolian world domination in the same way: "In heaven there is nobody but the one God, on earth there is nobody but the one Lord Genghis Khan, the son of God," he wrote to the pope in Rome.[4]

Monotheism and patriarchalism. Metaphysical monotheism found its echo not only in the political realm but also in the domination of men over women. In ancient matriarchal cultures there are traces to be found everywhere that the "Great Mother," the "Mother of All," "Mother earth," was honored.[5] These cults had a pantheistic character. The divine is that eternally fruitful life, creative matter itself (*natura naturans*). All individual phenomena arise out of the great stream of life and are finally returned into it out of which they will be reborn.

Monotheism, by contrast, is the religion of patriarchy. It can actually still be discerned on many Greek temple sites just how the "father of the universe" Zeus suppressed and subjugated the earth mother, Gaea. In this way the dominion of the man over woman and family was legitimized. The father of the family (*pater familias*) represented the divine authority of the heavenly omnipotent Father in the home, exactly as the "father of the fatherland," the emperor (*pater patriae*), represented this authority in the political realm. The monotheistic Lord-God was always, and remains, the masculine God, the almighty. He determines everything, but is determined by nothing else. He is loved by all but he loves only himself: a heavenly narcissus.[6] He stands over against the world as its Creator, Lord, and Judge. Nature is the "work of his hands" but is in no way an emanation of his own nature. The patriarchal theologies in Christianity have presented God, to this day, according to the images of the man as fatherly omnipotence, whenever they reduced God to "the Almighty."[7]

Monotheism and the subjugation of the body. Monotheism found its correspondence not least in the understanding of individual humans and their relationships to themselves. The "soul dominating the body" (*anima forma corporis*) corresponds to the God who dominates the world. Humans are the image of God on earth as far as they are subjects who can say, "I am, I know, and I will." Insofar as humans are in self-possession, are at their own disposal, and are continually their own possibility, they correspond to God. This understanding of human subjectivity comes from Augustine. For him, in good Neoplatonic style, the soul is the best part of the person because it is elevated above the body. The soul animates the body and dominates it, using it as a tool. The soul affects the body, but the body can exert no influence on the soul in return. It is the soul which is the God-related part of the human. "Nothing is mightier than that creature which is called the reasonable spirit." "When you are in the Spirit, you are in the middle; when you look downward, there is the body; when you look upward, God is there."[8] Augustine therefore named this body-dominating soul (i.e., the reasonable spirit that rules its world) the image of God in humans. The subjugated body cannot be pointed to as the image of God (*imago Dei*) but is instead only a trace of God (*vestigia Dei*). Because the soul is ultimately the active subject in every single human being, all humans are in themselves the image of God on earth. Such is the content of Augustine's psychological doctrine of the Trinity. In summary, through spirit, knowledge, and love, or through memory, understanding, and will, each individual corresponds to God.[9]

THE DOCTRINE OF THE TRINITY: GOD'S LORDSHIP OR GOD'S COMMUNITY?

The Christian doctrine of God distinguishes itself throughout in that, following Christ and for Christ's sake, it speaks, and must speak, of the Triune God. The doctrine of the Trinity is that specifically Christian element in the concept of God. Does this trinitarian element win against the metaphysical, political, patriarchal, and psychological monotheisms, or is it suppressed by them? This is not only a question that will be answered theologically in the doctrine of God; it is at the same time a question that will be answered in anthropology, for it concerns the meaning and understanding of life.[10] In the theology of the Eastern church, a monarchical doctrine of the Trinity was developed: The Father exercises the monarchy in the Deity itself, for he is the causeless Cause of the Son and Spirit. The Son and the Spirit are like the two hands of the one Father.

The theology of the Western church developed a trinitarian doctrine of the monarchy: The divine Trinity, operating *ad extra* in creation and redemption, is always undivided and is one Subject. As a result, God works in a trinitarian way inwardly only; outwardly, however, God acts monotheistically.[11]

In both conceptions, the doctrine of the one Lordship of God—as dominion in super-power—has triumphed over against the doctrine of the three persons in God, the divine Trinity. To this day the development of the doctrine of the Trinity has not led to any essential revision of this monarchical monotheism. Even recent contributions toward a doctrine of the Trinity in Karl Barth and Karl Rahner have brought, in this regard, no innovation. They both subordinate the doctrine of the Trinity to the doctrine of God's Lordship and use this view in such a way as to secure the sovereignty of God over against human beings. The "self-revelation" of God "as the Lord" is the root of Barth's doctrine of the Trinity. The "self-communication" of God has a threefold structure, says Karl Rahner.[12]

The monarchical doctrines of the Trinity have thus changed very little of the domination of the human over nature, of the man over woman, and of the soul over the body. Instead, they have stabilized and legitimized these relationships of domination.

What is the price and who are the victims of these doctrines of montheistic domination? The first victim is God. If God is understood only as one who dominates, God will be cut off and isolated from the fullness of life. The "Almighty" can do all things but may not display any weakness. God may rule but cannot suffer. God must direct but cannot be directed. God must always speak but cannot listen. A God who is so one-sidedly defined, simply cannot be the living God. This God has become an idol, an idol of power and domination. The obverse characteristics, severed from God, become then the characteristics of the subjugated and the dominated: suffering, passion, obedience, following, sensitivity, and feeling. The God who alone is active and all-causative condemns all others to passivity and utter dependence.

The second victims are human beings. This separation of God from every other thing shows itself also in God's image on earth: The boy brought up to "be a man" learns to suppress his feelings, to repress his instincts, and to master his body. In this way he is brought up to "lord" it over the woman, for whom the separated side of life includes her "given" characteristics: feeling, instinct, sensuality, and corporeity.[13]

If ultimately the body-dominating soul becomes the only explanation of the image of God, then separation and subjugation are imposed on every person. The wholeness of human life is lost.[14]

For that reason, we want to strike out in the opposite direction. We will seek to present the specifically Christian element in the doctrine of God (i.e., the doctrine of the Trinity) not from the perspective of the external Lordship of God (*Herrschaft Gottes*) but from that of the internal community of God (*Gemeinschaft Gottes*). We see the nature of this Triune God in God's unity. We know God's healing work through the unifying of humanity and all that is separated and segregated on earth into the divine community.

We will discover God's image on earth in human life together with nature, in the community of men and women, and in the wholeness of body, soul, and spirit in human existence. We therefore want to develop a social doctrine of the Trinity and, with it, an anthropology of the image of God that expresses solidarity, wholeness, and mutuality.

The Correlation Between the Doctrine of the Trinity and Human Community

For a long time the theological tradition has given priority to the unity, and thus to the Lordship, of God, over the Triune God.[15] The unity of the Triune God consisted of the one homogeneous divine nature. This was Tertullian's well-known formula: "One substance, three persons" (*una substantia, tres personae*). Since the beginning of the modern era in Europe, God is thought of not simply as the highest substance, but simultaneously also as the absolute Subject. As a result, the unity of God must also be defined differently. This unity is now to be identified in the identical divine Subject. This is "the personal God." From this comes the formulation of the modern doctrine of the Trinity: one divine Subject, three modes of being. In this formula, too, the unity of God is given priority over Trinity.

We are able to go a step farther in that we discover the unity of the Triune God in the uniquely singular character of the community shared by the three persons themselves. In English the expression Tri-une expresses the intention of this very clearly: three persons, one community. (In the German, the expression *Drei-einigkeit* captures this same intention.)

The Tri-une God presents a unique community which is decisive for all life in God's name, because all life in that name has been drawn into this eternal divine community. From this we want to take up three basic concepts of the Trinity and see what they say to the understanding of the human community, because they are nothing else but the basic concepts of community: (1) person, (2) relation, (3) community (*perichoresis*).

1. The expression *persona* originally meant "mask" and came from the language of the theater. The intention was to indicate the presence of a disguise through which the actor's voice comes. In contemporary usage the sociological concept of role corresponds exactly to that of the theater mask, and it is used with regard to the social functions of people. The concept of person was probably first used in the modalistic doctrine of God, one God in three modes of appearance. In Greek theology, however, the expression *hypostasis* was used in order to understand Father, Son, and Spirit. *Hypostasis* expresses concrete unique being. The inclusion of this meaning in Latin theology fundamentally changed the concept of person. As in our speech today, person no longer connotes interchangeable masks and social roles, but refers instead to nontransferable, unique, individual concrete being (*Dasein*): *rationalis naturae individua substantia* (Boethius). This transformation of the person-concept from within the Christian doctrine of the Trinity has had wide-ranging anthropological consequences. It has led to an understanding of the human personality with unalienable human rights and has overcome anthropological modalism, which dissolves the person into his or her social functions.

2. Now the three divine persons are not there simply for themselves. They are there in that they are there for one another. They are persons in social relationship. The Father can be called Father only in relationship with the Son; the Son can be called Son only in relationship with the Father. The Spirit is the breath of the one who speaks. The breath goes out from the Father in the eternal moment in which the Father speaks the Word, which in another relationship is called the Son. Three divine persons exist, therefore, in their inexchangeable personal being (*Personsein*), for and with one another, determined in and through their relationships to one another. Being-a-person (*Personsein*) means "being in relationship." This relational understanding of the person was elaborated by Augustine. It would be a relapse into modalism, however, if one were simply to replace "person" with "relationship," and instead of three persons to speak of three relationships in God—fatherhood, sonhood, and spirituality. Person and relation are equally original.

Richard of St. Victor deepened the concept of relationship by means of the concept of ec-sisting. Ec-sisting means "being out of oneself," which is an experience of oneself in the ecstasy of love. To be totally in the other and to understand oneself totally from the other is this ecstasy of love. In the power of mutual love the Father ec-sists totally in the Son, and the Son in the Father.

It was Hegel who carried this line of thought one step further: personal being (*Personsein*) means to dispose of oneself to others and to come in others to oneself. This deepening of the concept of relationships in the Christian doctrine of the Trinity can lead to an understanding of the *social character (Sozialität)* of the human person. The western European individualism could have been avoided had God been understood in trinitarian rather than theistic terms.

3. Once we have perceived the divine persons in their mutual relationships, we must ask about the unity of the Tri-une God. Does the unity of the persons lie in the common divine nature they possess? Does their unity lie in the one divine Lordship they execute? These possibilities are introduced into the Trinity from outside and are not conceptions of unity that emerge out of the Trinity itself. When the three persons exist in the power of their relationships with one another, for each other and in each other, then they themselves shape their own unique unity, namely, as a tri-unity. John of Damascus grasped this unity with his doctrine of the eternal *perichoresis* as the unique union of the three persons. That is to say, the divine community is shaped by the mutual relationships of the divine persons themselves.

The tri-unity is a unity of a special kind. It is this unity that is sought by humans in their community with one another, is anticipated and foreshadowed in their love toward one another, and is experienced in the ecstasy of joy and gratitude and in moments of mystical unity. The divine Trinity is so inviting and so strong that the divine life reflects itself in true human community and takes human community up into itself, "that they may be all one; even as thou, Father, art in me, and I in thee, that they also may be in us [John 17:21]." That means nothing other than that the human community is to be the image of the Triune God on earth. Not only human beings as single persons and not only the persons in social relationship to one another, but the human community as a whole

Giovanni Spague, Trinity

in all its facets shall and can correspond to the divine life of the Triune God. God wills to recognize and reflect the divine self in human community as in a mirror. A community that corresponds to the Triune God is a community in which, except for their personal characteristics, people will share everything: "They had everything in common" and "There was not a needy person among them [Acts 4:32, 34]." Property belongs to the world of dead things; community is the life of God.

THE SOCIAL IMAGE OF GOD

In order to understand the secret of the Triune God, Christian theology throughout its history has taken up two differing analogies: the analogy of the individual person and the analogy of community. The first analogy led to the psychological doctrine of the Trinity in the West. The other analogy led to the social doctrine of the Trinity in the East.

Gregory of Nazianzus found the analogy and thus the image of the Triune God in the original nuclear family, Adam, Eve, and Seth.[16] Rather than the human individual in itself, it is this primal cell of human community which corresponds to the Triune God. These three persons are from one flesh and blood, and they are one family. In the human nuclear family the Triune God recognizes the divine self.

Augustine opposed this social analogy, calling it depraved.[17] If this analogy were correct, he pointed out, then a man could be the image of God only when he had found a wife and had a child with her. But where scripture speaks of the image of God, it means only man and woman; there is no mention of the child Seth in the creation narrative. Paul settles the matter (1 Corinthians 11:7) when he names only the man as "the image and glory of God" and the woman only as "the glory of man." Insofar as the woman shares human nature with the man, she is, with the man, the image of God; but insofar as her destiny is to be his helper, she cannot in herself be the image of God. The man, of course, alone and of himself is the image of God. There are two different consequences for Augustine. First, that the image-of-God character is sexless and is to be found in the reasonable soul of every human being. Second, that the woman can be known as the image of God only when she is subordinate to the man as her head.

Michael Schmaus calls this a "profound and intelligent solution."[18] To me it seems "spirit-less" (geistlos), in the literal sense of the word, because it is a solution without the "community of the Holy Spirit." Of course, the image of the original nuclear family of Adam, Eve, and Seth is easily misunderstood. Family status can hardly be the measure by which the image of God is tested. Nevertheless, the existence of the anthropological triangle remains; every human is either woman or man and child or his or her parents. With woman and man the social character (Sozialität) of the human race is designated, and with parent and child its procreativity is designated. The one is the human community in space, the other is the human community in time. When the whole human is determined by the image of God, then human social character must be understood with regard to the sexes and to the generations. Human community is simultaneously the community of sexes and the community of generations.

Augustine could evade this social analogy only by a limiting of the image of God to the soul and by abstracting the soul from the body. That in so doing he disqualified not only the corporeal but also the woman shows that he did not escape from the social analogy. He could only distort it in a masculine way.

The community of the sexes and of the generations is primarily the whole image and is in total correspondence with the Triune God insofar as these become a community of solidarity, overcoming their inhuman malformations.

The social analogy of the nuclear family throws its own light in another way back onto the Trinity. If the woman, man, and child are the image of God on earth, then eternal Fatherhood, eternal Motherhood, and eternal Childhood are discovered in the Triune God.[19] One discovers the Motherhood of the Holy Spirit. Like Wisdom (chokma), the Spirit (ruach, according to its Hebraic origin) is feminine in nature.[20] In the Kabbalistic tradition the Spirit was valued as the "feminine principle" in the Deity.[21]

The power of the Spirit—She—was made masculine for the first time by translation into Latin and Germanic thought. Even in Western Christianity, however, the knowledge of the Spirit's feminine

Trinity with Female Holy Spirit

character always remained. The symbol of the dove is feminine, for example. This knowledge was alive especially in those Christian churches in which women and men were actively and consciously included within the community. And so Count Zinzendorf proclaimed the motherhood of the Holy Spirit in 1741 at the founding of the community of brothers and sisters in Bethlehem, Pennsylvania:

> This is the . . . divine family on earth: The Father of our Lord Jesus Christ is our true Father, and the Spirit of Jesus Christ is our true Mother, because the Son of the living God . . . is our true Brother. The Father must love us and can do no other, the Mother must guide us and can do no other, and the Son, our brother, must love our soul as his own soul, our body as his own body, because we are flesh of his flesh and bone of his bone, and he can do no other.[22]

The concept of the Motherhood of the Holy Spirit comes from the Syrian church fathers. Makarios said in his homilies: "The Spirit is our Mother, because the Paraclete, the Comforter, will comfort us as a mother her child (Isa. 66:13) and because the believers are 'reborn' out of the Spirit and are thus children of the mysterious mother, the Spirit (John 3:3,5)."[23]

This discovery of the Motherhood of the Holy Spirit leads to a social understanding of the image of God. To express that in the opposite way, it will be possible to arrive at a real social understanding of the image of God only when the feminine character of the Spirit is recognized. This is not simply a matter of changing metaphors; it concerns, far more, the restitution of femininity in the dignity of the image of God. Only then will also actual masculinity be seen in its original dignity, and this masculinity will no longer appear with the distorting character of domination.

Here then an appreciation for the wholeness of the human being is opened up. Both soul and body are incorporated into this wholeness, with the body, so long suppressed by the Neoplatonic-Augustinian doctrine of the soul dominating the body, being taken up into the glory of the image of God. The total human person as child, as woman, and as man is the image of God on earth. Corporeal life is the clear image and not simply the indistinct "trace of God" in the world. Otherwise, the body could not become "the temple of the Holy Spirit," as Paul says. "The body is . . . meant for the

Lord, and the Lord for the body. . . . So glorify God in your body
[1 Cor. 6:13, 20]."

The Holy Trinity as Social Program

"The Holy Trinity is our social program." This sentence is present
in the nineteenth century in the work of such very different theologians as the Orthodox Nikolai Fyodorov, the Anglican Frederick
Denison Maurice, and the Lutheran Nikolai Grundtvig.[24] They saw
in the special unity of the Triune God the primal image of real
human community—initially in the church and then also in the
society. I want to identify with this theory and to illustrate the thesis
with the content of my thought developed to this point.

The knowledge of God and knowledge of the human stand together in a correlation. That has been shown in the opposition
between monotheism and the doctrine of the Trinity—the doctrine
of dominating Lordship and the doctrine of liberating community.
Concepts developed in the doctrine of God and in anthropology act
reciprocally on one another.

In the doctrine of God in the Western church, the notion of
interdependence is seen above all in the concept of person. This
has left an enduring impression on the Western European understanding of the human. Today when we see the indivisible and
unalienable qualities of the human personality and thus protect these
by means of human rights and civil law, we are able to thank the
trinitarian concept of person.

But why was the concept of social relations not developed with
equal force? Such a development would have prevented the fall
from personalism to individualism. This development did not take
place precisely because the doctrine of the Trinity was changed into
the monotheism of the one almighty God. In order to emulate this
God, the human being (i.e. the man) became more and more defined
and determined by power and the will to power. The will to power
and the arrogance of power became the obsession, the God complex,
of modern men.

Why wasn't the concept of trinitarian unity developed with the
same force? Precisely because the unity of the Triune God has since
Augustine been defined not in a trinitarian way but rather mono-

El Greco, The Trinity (1541-1614)

theistically as the one divine nature or the one divine Lordship. These concepts, therefore, remained ineffective, even though they would have provided a suitable basis for establishing the social relationships both of the person and of the community of humans one with the other and with nature.

The social doctrine of the Trinity is thus in a position to overcome monotheism in the concept of God and individualism in anthropology by developing simultaneously a social personalism and a personal socialism. How important that is for the divided world in which we live and think!

Considered from the point of view of religion, the personalism of the Western world is monotheistically stamped. Because of this it is perverted again and again to individualism. The socialism of the Eastern world, however, is on the other hand not atheistic but pantheistic. Because of this it reverts ever again to collectivism. Social personalism and personal socialism could be brought theologically to a point of convergence with the help of the social doctrine of the Trinity.

That which alone corresponds to the Triune God is one united and uniting Christian congregation without domination and subjugation, and one united and uniting humanity without class domination and tyrannical oppression. That is the world in which humans are destined by their social relationships and not by their power or property. That is the world in which humans have all things in common and share all things one with another—all, that is, except their personal characteristics.

The Triune God who is the communal God must ultimately be understood as the living God who breaks through human isolation and religious divisions. This God comes in Jesus as the Brother next to us. We come to face him as the Abba-Father of Jesus, and we live out of our Mother, the Spirit. The whole human person in complete community with other human persons lives before, with, and out of the whole God.

Let me conclude by pointing to visible symbols: The ritual of domination is subjugation; the ritual of community is embracing.

Elisabeth and Jürgen Moltmann

BECOMING
HUMAN
IN NEW
COMMUNITY

7

Becoming Human in New Community

I

ELISABETH:
Church history begins when a few women set out to pay their last respects to their dead friend Jesus. It begins when, contrary to all reason and all hope, a few women identify themselves with a national traitor and do what they consider to be right, what in their eyes equals quality of life, namely, loving one who sacrificed his life, never abandoning him as dead. Church history begins when Jesus comes to them, greets them, lets them touch him just as he had touched and restored them in their lives. Church history begins when the women are told to share with the men this experience, this life they now comprehend, this life their hands have touched.

This chapter was presented first at the WCC Consultation on the Community of Women and Men in the Church, held in Sheffield, UK, June 1981, and later as one of the Earl Lectures in Berkeley, California, in February 1982. It is reprinted from *The Ecumenical Review*, Vol. 33, No. 4, Oct. 1981, by permission of the World Council of Churches.

This story as told by Matthew is generally known as the Easter appearance to the women but never as the beginning of church history. Officially, church history begins with the mission of the men apostles and, officially, no women are present on that occasion. Right up to the present time many churches have traced their origin back to this apostolic succession. Almost all the leaders of these churches are male and depend mostly on males for their order and their ideas. The idea of God is conceived mainly in masculine terms: male leadership roles are used to describe what God does—God reigns, judges, governs; what God is corresponds to what men would like to be—judge, king, ruler, army commander. In the process, women's experiences of Jesus have been forgotten—Jesus as a friend who shares their life and is ever near them, a friend who offers them warmth and tenderness in their loneliness and powerlessness. The feminist movement in the Western world has given many women the courage to discover themselves, to express again their own religious experiences, to read the Bible with fresh eyes and to rediscover their original and distinctive role in the gospel. For these women feminism is not a white, Western, bourgeois movement but one deeply rooted in the gospel.

In the social upheavals and cultural crises of the last fifteen years many other groups have made the painful discovery that God is on the side of patriarchy. Above all, God has become a stranger to many women in the Western world. It is no longer possible for them to reconcile God with their conceptions of life and with their identity. Certainly, patriarchy is not to be blamed on the men. Men should not feel or be held personally responsible for it. Patriarchy is a cultural form dating back thousands of years, and many cultural and economic achievements of our world would have been inconceivable without it. But, essentially in the last two centuries, disastrous associations with colonialism and racism, capitalism and sexism, have arisen out of patriarchy, leading us to start seeking the fundamental causes of these evils. In the process it has become alarmingly clear that colonialism, capitalism, racism, and sexism have been supported, justified, and even religiously glorified by a patriarchal Christianity. "Gott mit uns" ("God with us") were the words inscribed on every German soldier's belt-buckle in the First World War. In the name of a triumphal, social-reforming God, people were enslaved, workers exploited, and women taught to hold

110

their peace. And only minority groups of Christians protested against all this.

Today women are once again setting out to discover life, to enliven all that has become dead, to know Jesus as the one he once was for them. They are seeking to liberate themselves from the patriarchal domination in which their thinking was done for them as well as for others considered to be not fully adult. They want to free themselves from being treated like children, to be free from the tutelage which denies them any say at all, or allows them only a limited say, in society. They no longer want to accept the values imparted by the patriarchal world system—either for themselves or for their children or for society as a whole.

What do women want?

I would like to take a little time to consider this question, for many people even in the church are afraid of women. Men are afraid that women hate them, women are afraid of women who could cause their traditional roles to become insecure. There is a fear of any kind of radicalism which supposedly is not in harmony with the love of Christ. What women want is a new community in which those with power begin to listen to those without power. A community where there are opportunities for the powerless to express themselves and get organized. A community in which power is redistributed and those in power learn to give up their power—for the sake of justice. Women want a community which is not obsessed with profit and economic growth but concerned with the basic needs of all human beings. They are able to stand up for all this passionately and credibly because they have first-hand experience of what it is like to be treated like children, to be in tutelage, without rights, to live a life at second-hand (the husband's or the man's), to give life but to be allowed to fashion it only within a limited domestic circle and not in society as a whole.

What women want is a whole life, one which embraces body, soul, and spirit, no longer compartmentalized into private and public spheres; a life, moreover, which fills them with a trust and hope transcending biological death.

This seems a huge and impossible utopian program. In the last analysis, however, it is simply taking seriously what can be read in the prophet Isaiah's visions of peace and a part of what the apostle Paul once recognized, in a flash of inspiration, namely, that in Christ

111

there is neither Jew nor Greek, neither slave nor free, neither male nor female. It is also the old vision of the women which we find in the song of Miriam, one of the oldest passages in the Bible: trust in the God who has thrown horse and rider—today we can say sex and domination—into the sea. This feminine tradition, which is found in many women's songs—of Hannah, of Deborah, Judith, and Mary's Magnificat—and which has always been with us, makes us keenly aware of what is happening in the world and what is going on within ourselves, in our bodies, in our souls, and in our spirits.

Women on the way to discover life.

Women in a church which is firmly in masculine hands.

In which direction lies the way? Certainly away from a patriarchy in which women have been oppressed, silenced, and are unable to speak for themselves. Away too from the church and its patriarchal structures? Away too from God, who—as Kate Millet said—was always tied to patriarchy or, to be more precise, was always occupied with patriarchy? For many women—even among us—this decision still has to be made.

Jürgen:

You have been asking: Is God on the side of patriarchy? Let me attempt to answer that by being self-critical and asking which God this is.

It was not Christianity that introduced patriarchy into the world. Patriarchy is a very ancient and widespread system of male domination. Christianity proved incapable of successfully opposing this system. Indeed, quite early on, Christianity was already taken over by men and made to serve patriarchy. This had a crippling effect on its liberating potential, as has been perceived by theologians of hope, liberation theologians, and political theologians in other contexts, when they criticized the "Constantinian captivity" of the church. It has now been fully demonstrated by feminist theology. The liberation of woman and then of man from patriarchy goes hand in hand, therefore, with a rediscovery of the freedom of Jesus and of the energies of the Holy Spirit. Leaving the monotheistic God of rulers and males behind us, we shall discover from the sources of Christianity the God who is in relationship, the God who can suffer, the uniting God, the God of fellowship and of community. This is the living God, the God of life, who was distorted through a pa-

112

triarchal system with its idols of power and domination. In this living God the male too will experience deliverance from the distortions which he himself has suffered and still suffers under patriarchy.

Oppression obviously has two sides. On the one side, there is the tyrant, on the other, the slave; here the dominating man and there the serving woman. Oppression destroys humanity on both sides. The oppressed person is robbed of humanity, and the oppressor becomes an inhuman monster. Both suffer alienation from their true nature, with the difference, of course, that one of them suffers in consequence, whereas the other appears to feel fine. On both sides, however, liberation from oppression is needed. But how is this possible for men, whose ideas and feelings are deeply influenced by patriarchy and who seem to enjoy their privileges?

The starting point for us men, just as it is for you women, is to become aware of the real situation and to realize the extent to which patriarchy cheats us out of the blessings of true life. Each man can achieve this anamnesis for himself by asking how he was trained as a child to "become a man," what feelings he was expected to suppress, what instincts he had to control, what roles he was taught to adopt. He was trained to be a worker, a soldier, a father, a breadwinner, a conqueror, and a ruler. The first lessons he learned, therefore, were self-control and self-possession. He was terrified of becoming a "nothing," a "nobody," and ruled by the desire to "make something of himself."

Patriarchy cut the male in half. It split him into a subject, consisting of reason and will, and an object, consisting of heart, feelings, and physical needs. He had to identify himself with the former and keep his distance from the latter. This isolated the male and brought about a certain self-hatred. This division in the male is reflected and takes an aggressive form in the male subjugation and domination of the supposedly "frail," "emotional," and "physical" women. It is also reflected in the other reality that every ruler not only needs people at his command but also a throne to sit on. As can be seen from such symbols as Isis and Horus, Mary and the child Jesus, the throne on which the male ruler is seated is the mother. This division of the woman into mother and wife is a product of patriarchy. Unresolved mother-fixations and "machismo" vis-à-vis other women go together. There must be an end to both mothering and domination if the man is to become both free and mature.

113

The distress of the divided and isolated male is reflected in the majesty of the God of patriarchy. This God is the Almighty, the Ruler, the Absolute. This God determines everything and is not influenced by anything. This God is incapable of suffering. According to Aristotle, this God loves only the divine self and causes everything to accord with this self-love. If this God is assigned human traits, they are male traits. Knowledge of this God ascends from the family patriarch (*pater familias*) to the national patriarch (*pater patriae*), from the national patriarch to the patriarch of the church, and finally reaches the greatest patriarch, the Father of all in heaven (*omnipater*). And in the legitimation of authorities, one then descends from the heavenly Father of all downward. Between this heavenly Father of all and the mystery of Jesus' Abba-Father there is no connection. On the contrary, this God of patriarchy arises from the first division of the world into heaven and earth: heavenly father—mother earth.

The God of patriarchy is often portrayed through Christian forms in terms of the head and the body. The man is the head of the woman, Christ is the head of the man, God is the head of Christ (1 Corinthians 11:3). Only under the man as head is the woman in God's image, but not for herself alone (Augustine, Thomas Aquinas). He is the leader, she the led (Karl Barth).

The distress of the male Ruler-God lies in his lack of a name and his loneliness. He is defined only by his function as ruler and proprietor of the world. Who he himself is remains unknown. Thus patriarchy divides, separates, and isolates God. A God who is no more than "the Almighty" is not a God but a monster. Any man who emulates this God becomes a hapless beast; he is no more than an expression of the will to power. Since the modern, white male became afflicted with this "God complex" (H.E. Richter), patriarchy has ceased to be a source of order and protection and has instead become a source of destruction and fear.

You said that women today are on the way to discover life, a life which is whole and one of community. Men who wish to discover life for themselves and then in community with women must shake off the pressure of patriarchy as they would some nightmare and eliminate these suppressions of true life, so as to become full human beings. What happens to us here is rather like what happened to the disciples who hear the women's Easter message and then, half

114

believing, half disbelieving, go off to find for themselves the living Lord whom they had forsaken shortly before his crucifixion. In this common "resurrection-movement," we men could discover "the new community of women and men," which delivers us from patriarchal distortions and opens up to us the wholeness of human life.

ELISABETH:

Both men and women are crippled, but in different ways and with different consequences. You still cling to the throne of Isis even though we no longer want to be the mothers who carry Horus.

Women today, therefore, should lead the way to a new community of women and men. They should do so, not so much in order to make good the discrimination they have suffered and the injustice that has been inflicted on them. This precedence of women need not be humiliating for men. They should see it more as an opportunity to leave women room to discover and point out the obstacles along the way. For only in this way can a sustainable community grow.

Since we began to discover what *our* life is, our life as women, our life in solidarity with all the women in the world who suffer discrimination, our spiritual life, our life as Christian women, a life which we want to take hold of, feel, endure, change, we have constantly come into collision with the barriers of our Christian tradition: our faith is the faith of the "fathers." Our religious testimonies are derived from a Bible edited by the patriarchs, obviously to the exclusion of any female participation in the process. Christian life is celebrated in our hymns in a paternalistic style. In our theology the man "leads" and the woman is "led" (Karl Barth). And when we inspect it in greater detail, we find that the tradition from which we are supposed to live is full to the brim of hostility to women. In any case, the life assigned to us as women is not a whole life. According to one biblical passage, we women are to be saved by childbearing, you men by faith. We are to hold our peace, you are permitted to speak. We tempted you and were the first to sin. But even if we turn a blind eye to these biblical blunders, the life assigned to women is a life at second-hand, life as supplementing that of the man, life from the Spirit and the Word but not life in the unity of body, soul, and spirit. In the distorted, patriarchalist view, our body has for far too long been considered embarrassing,

115

unclean, repulsive. In short, it is not life in its wholeness but a halved life.

Can the Christian tradition offer us any help to extricate ourselves from this halved life? Where do the sources and motivations exist for this in respect of our identity? What Christian traditions can accompany and support us on the way to wholeness? What Christian traditions can also help the man to be "whole" and give him an identity other than that of a patriarch?

JÜRGEN:

It is very true that the biblical, Christian, and church traditions were mainly written and edited by dominating men. At first sight, therefore, they provide little help for the liberation of the woman. History, it has been said, is always written by the victors. The oppressed have even been deprived of the conscious memorial of their own history of defeat and suffering. But these traditions "from above" can also be read, contrary to their intention, "from below." When we do this we discover in the histories of tyrants the suppressed histories also of the rebels against tyranny. In this sense, in and underlying the male history of the church there is also a history of Christian women, a female history of the church. To some extent, you yourself have rediscovered this history and found within it symbols and motifs that can lead women out of a divided life and into a whole life. Let me mention only three examples of these here:

1. For centuries, Christians have learned the story of the fall as it is told in the second account of creation (J), and told extremely graphically. This account also includes the first male disclaimer of guilt: "The woman whom thou gavest to be with me, she gave me fruit of the tree [Gen. 3:12]." Unfortunately, we find this in the New Testament as well: "For Adam was formed first, then Eve; and Adam was not deceived, but the woman was deceived and became a transgressor [1 Tim. 2:13-14]." This was used to prove woman's inferiority.

The story of the fall as told in the first account of creation in the Priestly tradition (P) was more or less forgotten. This tradition makes no mention of the apple, the woman, and the serpent, or of Adam— innocent if not very bright—but speaks of something quite different: "Now the earth was corrupt in God's sight, and the earth was filled

116

with violence [Gen. 6:11]." Of what did the corruption and sin consist? It consisted of the spread of violence among humans and animals. God therefore decided on the destruction of both in the flood. Evil and sin here are at their origin nothing other than violence, brutality, and "rape." Redemption means, therefore, a nonviolent life as commanded and promised by Jesus in the Sermon on the Mount. If we had paid heed to this account of creation, the myth of women's inferiority would not have arisen.

2. Women today ask sharply: "Is God a man?" In fact, the Christian doctrine of God is spoken of chiefly in male terms: Father, Son, and Holy Spirit. Is this really true, though? There is an ancient but suppressed tradition of the maternal office of the Holy Spirit, the divine motherhood. The Christian communities that were subsequently driven out of the mainline men's church found it natural to speak of the Spirit as the mother of Jesus. In Ethiopian pictures of the Trinity, the Spirit is depicted as a mother. The nuclear family Adam, Eve, and Seth was often used by the Greek church fathers, too, as an image of the Triune God on earth, which certainly presupposes that the Holy Spirit is female and archetype of the mother. Nor was it mere chance that Count Zinzendorf rediscovered the maternal office—the motherhood—of the Holy Spirit when founding the Pennsylvania community of brothers and sisters in 1741: "This is the divine family on earth . . . for the Father of our Lord Jesus Christ is our true Father, the Spirit of our Lord Jesus Christ is our true Mother, because the Son of the living God is our true brother."

Personally I find this idea helpful not only because it discovers the female principle in the Godhead but also because it picks up an element of the truth in pantheism. If the Spirit is our mother, then I am able to feel that I am not only "under God" but also "in God." This idea delivers me from one-sided monotheistic father images of God and helps me to experience the whole God with my whole being. It helps me to find the community God in our own community.

3. Finally, it seems to me that the undoubtedly difficult and abstract development of the doctrine of the Trinity in the Christian concept of God was nevertheless already itself paving the way for victory over the masculine ruler God. It is true, of course, that

117

"Trinity" sounds just like something out of the abstract male theology "from above." What I mean by it, however, is the mysterious whole by which our whole life is embraced.

There is always a mutual interaction between knowledge of God and our self-knowledge. The theology of the Western church located the divine image of humanity in our "reasonable soul," which governs the body. By its control over itself and over the earth, humanity—that is, the male—corresponds to the ruler God. Individualism in the view of humanity and monotheism in the view of God are twin-born.

Since we know today that humanity constitutes a unity of body, soul, and spirit and finds its salvation in experiencing the wholeness of life, it cannot be only the human soul which is the divine image on earth. Humanity itself in its bodily nature, humanity itself in the community of women and men, corresponds to God. To which God? There can be only one answer: to the God in relationship, the unifying God, the God of community, that is, the Triune God. The rule of this God is not divide and conquer (*divide et impera*); the Triune God is present, rather, in the uniting of the divided and in the healing of what is separated and torn into pieces. The mighty man may be an imitation of the Almighty, but only a human community in which human beings have all things in common and share all things, irrespective of individual characteristics, can be an image of the Triune God. This thought helps me personally to seek God not only in heaven above, not only in the inward depths of the soul, but also and above all between us in our community.

You asked: What can help us to liberate ourselves from our divided life? What Christian traditions can help us along the way to wholeness? Our traditions are always a collection of past hopes and past experiences. These have their value, but it is only a limited value. No tradition can settle the future. At best, traditions can prepare the way into the future. What the Spirit itself creates is always something new and always full of surprises. The Spirit is not tied to the traditions but takes from them that which points the way to the future. Christianity is more than a tradition; it is a hope.

ELISABETH:

Many women will still find it difficult to rediscover themselves in the female correlations of male conceptions of God. What they are really asking is whether we women should rediscover our identity in male symbols—supplemented by feminine ideals.

They will put more trust in their own imaginations than in the tradition. They are already developing their own language: God is the baker woman. Jesus can be their sister. They can pray: "Our Father-Mother in heaven. . . ." Feminist theology—its very name sends shivers up the spine of many theologians!—is for many women the only way they can speak freely and discover themselves to be daughters of God. Women have a culture of their own. It is still very different in the different countries in Asia and in Africa. It is a more concrete and pictorial culture than the corresponding male culture in each case, though it is often buried underground. For us, therefore, theo-fantasy takes its place alongside theo-logy and frequently reexcavates the buried sources.

For theology, largely commandeered by men, what matters most is that it should take seriously not only past experiences and traditions but also contemporary and coming experiences and traditions—theo-fantasy. Life—including Christian life—is much more diverse and colorful than any written tradition. What will be important here is that men learn to listen and to sit at the feet of women, as Mary sat at the feet of Jesus.

II

ELISABETH:

A new community can mature and bear fruit only if women remain autonomous human beings. The contribution they can make to community will not be a vital and lively one unless they retain their singularity, specificity, distinctiveness as women. The life women have been looking for and have now rediscovered will become everyone's common concern only if they continue to make it their cause.

Many find that statement difficult and paradoxical, women as well as men. We are used to thinking of the church as a great big loving family in which everyone is self-effacing for the sake of the others, forgetful of self in the interests of a great cause. Everyone and everything should be united in one great first-person plural—one great "we."

119

If women and men are to come together in a new community, they must say good-bye to such wishful thinking. They must each separately accept the pain of division and even the possible deprivation of love. They can discover themselves, in their wholeness with all its unexplored possibilities.

Many women in the church may find this particularly hard to accept, for they have gotten used to sacrificing themselves readily, taking a back seat; it has become almost second nature to accept that this is their Christian life-style. Men find it hard because they have gotten used to working with women who are always eager to help and because, by virtue of their official rank in the churches and the power that goes with it, the men have turned the cause of Jesus into a patriarchy of love. We have to relearn what loving means; we must learn a love that makes others mature instead of smothering them or glorifying them, a love that creates an area in which there is no domination.

The responsibility that men have become accustomed to assume and the renunciation that women have become accustomed to practice are patterns of behavior which derive from a strict allocation of sex roles. The life of our churches is based on patriarchal patterns of behavior from which no new community can possibly grow today. Women have begun to free themselves from these roles. How are the men to be liberated from these roles?

JÜRGEN:

Before I come to the question of the church, I should try to develop one point a little further. It is the men who are mainly "disconcerted" by women who emancipate themselves from age-old subjection. Women should not cover this fact up out of love, nor should we men deny it out of pride. We are becoming insecure in the masculine roles that have been instilled into us. We have to relearn everything, and every existential experience of relearning is painful. But the problem lies still deeper. The man also feels that his manly pride is violated. His sense of self-respect is shaken. His patriarchal identity disintegrates. He no longer knows who he really is. One reaction to this is aggression. But the most common reaction is depression.

Women are experiencing their new identity, their dignity, and their liberation into complete humanity. Men find it difficult to follow them in this way because, to discover the starting point for

120

their liberation into complete humanity, they have first of all to return deep into themselves. They have to break through the hard crusts of their alienation in order to reach the core of their human nature. Moreover, man must abandon self-righteousness if he is to learn to trust his humanity. To put it simply, the ruling "lord" in man must die so that the brother can be born, ready for honest friendship.

For men this also means no longer identifying themselves with the male caste but instead breaking out of the male code. To do so may earn them contempt and they can become lonely. In the education of the child to "manhood," the male caste has always played the leading part. It also brands its dissenters as "traitors."

Any man who is willing to abandon the masculine privileges conferred on him by the patriarchal society must also learn to abandon his male responsibility for the so-called "weaker sex." The "noble," "knightly," and "gentlemanly" overtones of this morality make its abandonment particularly difficult for many of us. But men who welcome and respect the coming of age of the woman must also learn to limit and to give up this "responsibility" feeling.

III

ELISABETH:

The churches sometimes seem to me just like these men's associations. Can they possibly cope today when so many women who have been kept in tutelage are "coming of age"? Is the church prepared to take seriously these women who have rediscovered their subjectivity? And by "taking them seriously" I mean recognizing their rights and according them power. This subjectivity is potentially explosive; it could produce an explosion of previously pent-up creativity. It has implications for many church traditions. It calls in question religious images and forms of church life. Many women today are saying, "We are the church." Does their way lead to a new community of men and women?

JÜRGEN:

The Christian church finds it particularly difficult to limit responsibility clearly. The reason for this is that, in the church, the supreme values are service, care, sacrifice for others, and therefore responsibility. This mild dictatorship of love, this "patriarchy of love," as you call it, is very difficult to escape from. Are not Christians always on active service, and do they not exist only "for others"? I also used to believe that, but not any more. It now seems to me to be actually false and a concealed form of domination. Christians are in the first place simply "with others." Only as those who delight in life with others do they then, when need arises, also sacrifice themselves "for others." Their love comes up against its boundary in the autonomy of others. Not even Jesus came to fetter human beings to himself by his ministry, to make himself indispensable for them. "Your faith has saved you," he habitually says when people want to thank him for being healed. Your *own* faith! God exists "for us" only in our distress, for it is God's will to live "with us" in eternity. God wants us as "autonomous human beings," as you rightly said.

As long as a church regards itself as a "servant church," as a "church for the nation" or a "church for the world" or "a church for others," it will always regard the subjectivity and adulthood of those it "cares for" as a threat to itself. Only when this "caring-from-above" church becomes a community of the people will it welcome the autonomous subjectivity of women, of workers, of disabled people, as energy of the Spirit. In the established churches there are few women pastors and no women bishops. But in many basic communities in Latin America, the leadership of women is a matter of course. Up to the present, only persecuted communities and basic communities have experienced the full range of charismata in the free community of men and women, a community without above and below. Paradoxically enough, it will be from "below" that the Spirit will come into the established male churches. We should look for the Spirit where human beings become autonomous agents of their own life and take the initiative for themselves.

IV

ELISABETH:

The power which is renewing women today in opposition to patriarchal structures and their own insecurity and discouragement, the power which liberates them and enables them to stand upright like the healed crippled woman, the power which enables them to discover their sisters, is the power of the Holy Spirit. For many women, the Spirit was for long enough something exceptional, miraculous. But many of them are now finding in the power of the Spirit that self-identification which the male church, the male God, the man Jesus, was unable to give them. They speak of the Holy Spirit as female, the Holy Spirit who in the language of Jesus really was also of the female gender. This is not something that is happening for the first time today. In the long history of the patriarchal church, women were able again and again to breach the dominant structures in the power of the Holy Spirit. But the church constantly distrusted both the women and the Spirit, condemning their works as extremism, heresy, paganism. The Holy Spirit was chained to official ministries and robbed of the renewing power.

Today—on the way to a new community—is it possible for us to begin trusting the Holy Spirit once again? The Spirit of extremists, crackpots, outsiders, visionaries, the Spirit of those who saw and touched life as did the women on Easter morning and whose reports seemed to the disciples as no more than idle tales? Can we—contrary to all reason—venture together on a new start in the name of this Spirit? Can the age-old suspicion and distrust of women—except when they speak cautiously, rationally, in a male language—be dispelled?

JÜRGEN:

Many find it hard to accept the feminist appeal to the Holy Spirit because they are not sure whether it is really the Holy Spirit or some other spirit they are appealing to. There have always been many different charismatic and spiritistic communities, inspired by a variety of spirits, not only the divine. Fearing the chaos of spirits, therefore, the church quite early in its history tied the Holy Spirit to the successive holders of the episcopal office, especially in the old doctrine of the monarchical episcopate. In addition, the Western church also tied the Spirit to the chain of Christology by means of the *filioque* clause in the Nicene Creed. The Spirit then becomes simply the internal subjective reality of Christ, of the word and sacraments of the church. No room is then left for the creatively new or for the surprises of the Holy Spirit, not even room to expect them.

If we are to be ready for the new and surprising work of the Holy Spirit, I suggest we differentiate more clearly between the *source of the Spirit* and the *criterion for discerning the spirits*.

The source of the Spirit is God, and what comes from this source is as colorful and diverse as creation itself. This is why when Christians in the New Testament speak of the Spirit they always speak in superlatives of the fullness, the richness, the inexhaustibility of the Spirit. This was how they themselves experienced the Spirit. Everyone had gifts of the Spirit in abundance. None suffered any lack here.

But the criterion for differentiating between the different spirits was for them the remembrance of the crucified Christ. Anything that could stand in the presence of the crucified Christ was divine Spirit. Anything that contradicted the crucified Christ, because it was the spirit of power or vanity, was rejected.

To come back to the story we began with, how did the women actually recognize the risen and living Christ? They might also have taken him for a ghost or some other figure. They recognized the risen Jesus at once because they had remained faithful to him right up to his death on the cross. They recognized him at once by the marks of the nails and from his way of dealing with them, familiar to them from experience. Nor is the life-giving Spirit to be recognized in any other way. The Spirit brings us into the liberating community of Jesus and brings Jesus into our midst in a uniting way.

Elisabeth:

One question I find inescapable: How did it happen that this experience of the women sank so soon without trace? How are we to explain the fact that almost two thousand years ago a viable community of women and men failed to materialize? Was it the fault of the women, who showed more confidence in the social structures than they did in themselves, obeyed men more than they did God, retreated into their ancient female roles and failed to trust in the renewing power of the resurrection? In our different countries and different churches we champion the cause of the women. Some of these women are struggling simply to survive; others are claiming

124

their right to be pastors or priests. It is a question of money, influence, teaching posts, a better social order. We live in different societies and have different assumptions.

There is one thing, it seems to me, which is important and which we all share: All of us need to begin again to trust ourselves and the renewing power of our religious experience; to trust our capacity to communicate life by all our senses and energies; not to give up in the face of overwhelming structures and never to lapse back again into an illegitimate obedience; to become ourselves again, in body, soul, and spirit, so that this spark may spread to men, to brothers and fathers, to mothers and children.

NOTES

1. Mary Magdalene—An Example of Patriarchal Distortion of History

1. Cf. here and following Leonard and Arlene Swidler, eds., *Women Priests* (New York: Paulist Press, 1977).
2. Cf. esp. Elizabeth Schussler-Fiorenza, "The Twelve," in ibid.
3. The following sections include material based on Elisabeth Moltmann-Wendel, *The Women Around Jesus: Reflections on Authentic Personhood* (New York: Crossroads, 1982).
4. Bernadette Brooten, "Junia, Outstanding Among the Apostles," in Swidler, *Women Priests*.
5. Raymond E. Brown, "Roles of Women in the Fourth Gospel," *Theological Studies* 36, no. 4 (1975).
6. Edgar Hennecke and Wilhelm Schneemelcher, *New Testament Apocrypha*, 2 vols. (Philadelphia: Westminster Press, 1966).
7. Ibid.
8. Ibid. See also apocryphal gospels discovered later, in Elaine Pagels, *The Gnostic Gospels* (New York: Vintage Books, 1981), pp. 76ff.

9. Jacobus de Varagine (1230-98), *The Golden Legend* (New York: Arno, 1941).

10. Cf. "Maria Magdalena," *Lexicon der Ikonografie* (Freiburg, 1974); also Marga Janssen, "Maria Magdalen in der Abendlandischen Kunst" (dissertation, Freiburg, 1961).

11. Gottfried Koch, *Frauenfrage und Ketzertum in Mittelalter* (Berlin: Akademie-Verlag, 1962).

12. Karl Künstle, *Ikonografie der christlichen Kunst* (Freiburg, 1926).

13. Hans Hansel, *Die Maria Magdalene Legende* (Bottrop, 1937).

14. Ibid.

15. Ibid.

16. *D. Martin Luthers Werke*. Kritische Gesamtausgabe (Weimar, 1883-), 28:449, 32, 35.

17. Ibid.

2. Martha—A Forgotten Medieval Tradition

1. Raymond E. Brown, "Roles of Women in the Fourth Gospel," *Theological Studies* 36, no. 4 (1975).

2. Johannes Leipoldt, *Die Frau in der antiken Welt und in Urchristentum* (Leipzig: Koehler & Amelang, 1954).

3. Rudolf Bultmann, *Das Evangelium des Johannes* (Göttingen, 1952), pp. 309ff. Available in English as *The Gospel of John: A Commentary* (Philadelphia: Westminster Press, 1971).

4. Cf. here and following in "Martha," *Lexikon der Ikonografie* (Freiburg, 1974); Germaine Maillet, "Sainte Marthe," in *L'Art et les Saints* (Paris, 1932).

5. C. Colafranchese, "Marta di Betania," in *Bibliotheca Sanctorum* (Rome, n.d.), 8:1216.

6. M. Bernards, *Speculum Virginum; Geistigkeit und Seelenleben der Frau im Hochmittelalter* (Cologne, 1955), pp. 194ff.

7. Jacobus de Varagine, *The Golden Legend* (New York: Arno, 1941).

8. Ibid., introduction by Richard Benz.

9. Erich Neumann, "Die Bedeutung des Erdarchetyps für die Neuzeit," *Eranosjahrbuch*, 1953; English summary follows article.

10. Edward H. Schaefer, *The Divine Woman: Dragon Ladies and Rain Maidens in T'ang Literature* (Berkeley: University of California Press, 1973).

11. Gottfried Koch, *Frauenfrage und Ketzertum im Mittelalter* (Berlin: Akademie-Verlag, 1962), p. 99.

12. Erich Neumann, *Die grosse Mutter* (Olten, 1974), p. 238. Available in English as *The Great Mother: An Analysis of the Archetype* (Princeton: Princeton University Press, 1974).

13. Frédéric Mistral, "Mireille," in *Frédéric Mistrals ausgewählte Werke* (Stuttgart, 1914), pp. 212ff. Available in English as *An English Version of Frédéric Mistral's "Mireio" from the original Provençal, under the Author's Sanction* (Avignon: J. Roumanille, 1867).

14. Neumann, "Die Bedeutung des Erarchetyps," p. 264.

15. Cf. "Matronae-Matres," in *Real-Encyclopädie der classischen Altertumswissenschaft* (Stuttgart, 1901), 14:2213ff.

16. Erich Jung, *Germanische Götter und Helden in Christlicher Zeit* (Munich and Berlin: J.F. Lehman, 1930), pp. 365ff.

17. Berthold Altaner, *Venturino von Bergamo, O.P. (1304-1346)* (n.p., n.d.).

18. *Un Santo Partiota, Il Beato Venturino da Bergamo*: Storie e Documenti (Rome, 1909), pp. 75ff.

19. Koch, *Frauenfrage und Ketzertum im Mittlelalter*.

20. Ibid.

21. For the following, cf. Maillet, "Sainte Marthe."

22. Johan Döllinger, *Beiträge auf Sektengeschichte des Mittelalters* (Munich: Beck, 1890), 2:381, 407, 411.

23. Mary Daly, *Beyond God the Father* (Boston: Beacon Press, 1973).

3. Christianity Between Patriarchy and Matriarchy

1. Mary Daly, *Beyond God the Father* (Boston: Beacon Press, 1973).

2. Letter to Harriet Visser't Hooft, in *Eva, Wo Bist Du?* (Gelnhausen: Hooft, 1981).

3. John Jacob Bachofen, *Dan Mutterrecht* (Stuttgart, 1861).

4. E.g., ibid., and R. Ranke-Graves, *Die weisse Göttin* (Berlin, 1981).

5. Hanna Wolff, *Jesus der Mann* (Stuttgart, 1975).

6. Merlin Stone, *When God Was a Woman* (New York: Harcourt Brace Jovanovich, 1978).

7. Ernst Harnischfeger, *Mystik im Barock* (Stuttgart: Urachhaus, 1980).

8. Ingrid Schlicher, "Weihnachten in der Bedeutung der Weiblichen Kulturgeschichte," *Frauenoffensive Journal*, 9 (January 1978).

9. Cf. Heide Göttner-Abendroth, *Die Göttin und ihr Heros* (Munich, 1981). She uses fairy tales and epics to show "matriarchal aftereffects in patriarchal societies" indicating "matriarchal opposition" within patriarchal societies.

4. God Means Freedom

1. Jean-Paul Sartre, *Existentialism and Humanism* (1948; reprint, Brooklyn: Haskell House, 1977).

2. Abraham Kuyper saw the struggle between divine authority and human freedom as the apocalyptic imprint of the modern world. Cf. "Reformation wider Revolution: Sechs Vorlesungen über den Calvinismus," *Stone Lectures* (Princeton: Princeton Theological Seminary, 1904).

3. Jan Milic Lochman, *Signposts to Freedom: The Ten Commandments and Christian Ethics* (1979; Minneapolis: Augsburg Publishing House, 1982).

4. Cf. R. Strunk, *Politische Ekklesiologie im Zeitalter der Revolution* (Munich, 1970); Jürgen Moltmann, *The Church in the Power of the Spirit* (San Francisco: Harper & Row, 1977), pp. 77ff.

5. With Jon Sobrino (*Christology at the Crossroads: A Latin-American Approach* [London, 1978]), I see liberation theologians moving in this direction, overcoming the secular theology they started from fifteen years ago.

6. Cf. M. Walzer, *The Revolution of the Saints: A Study in the Origins of Radical Politics* (London, 1965); Robert N. Bellah, *The Broken Covenant* (New York: Seabury Press, 1975); Robert Jewett, *The Captain America Complex* (Philadelphia: Westminster Press, 1974).

7. Cf. Louis Ginzberg, *The Legends of the Jews* (Philadelphia: Jewish Publication Society, 1956), 6:12, n. 60.

8. This is the thesis of my *The Crucified God* (New York: Harper & Row, 1974).

9. Cf. Jürgen Moltmann, "The Revolutions of Freedom: Christians and Marxists Struggle for Freedom," in *Religion, Revolution, and the Future* (New York: Charles Scribner's Sons, 1969), pp. 63-83; Daniel L. Migliore, *Called to Freedom: Liberation Theology and the Future of Christian Doctrine* (Philadelphia: Westminster Press, 1980).

10. The critique of "possessive individualism" is further developed by M. Douglas Meeks, "The Holy Spirit and Human Needs: Toward a Trinitarian View of Economics," *Christianity and Crisis*, November 10, 1980.

11. Christopher Lasch, *The Culture of Narcissism: American Life in an Age of Diminishing Expectations* (New York: W.W. Norton & Co., 1978).

12. Cf. Peter Kropotkin, *Gegenseitige Hilfe in der Tier- und Menschenwelt*, ed. G. Landauer (Leipzig, 1920). Available in English as *Mutual Aid: A Factor of Evolution* (New York: Knopf, 1925). This book by the Russian zoologist is a critique of Social Darwinism and certain aspects of Darwin's own writings.

13. Robert Benne and Philip Hefner, *Defining America: A Christian Critique of the American Dream* (Philadelphia: Fortress Press, 1974); Jürgen Moltmann, "Die 'Amerikanische Traum,'" *Evangelische Theologie* 37 (1977): 166-78.

14. E. Sarkisyanz, *Russland und der Messianismus des Orients: Sendungsbewusstsein und politischer Chiliasmus des Ostens* (Tübingen, 1955).

15. Paul Ricoeur, *Le Conflit des Interpretations: Essais d'Hermeneutique* (Paris, 1969), pp. 393ff. Available in English as *The Conflict of Inter-*

pretations: Essays in Hermeneutics (Evanston, IL: Northwestern University Press, 1974).

5. The Trinitarian Story of Jesus

1. Cf. Jürgen Moltmann, "The History of the Son," in *The Trinity and the Kingdom* (San Francisco: Harper & Row, 1981), pp. 61ff.
2. Adolf von Harnack, *What Is Christianity?* (San Francisco: Harper Torchbooks, 1957), p. 193.
3. Here I am following A. Schlatter, *Johannes der Taufer* (Basel: Reinhart, 1956); Walter Wink, *John the Baptist in the Gospel Tradition* (London, 1968); and Joachim Jeremias, *New Testament Theology* (New York: Charles Scribner's Sons, 1971).
4. Joachim Jeremias, *Abba* (Göttingen, 1966).
5. Cf. Martin Hengel, *The Son of God* (Philadelphia: Fortress Press, 1976), p. 63: "Even if Jesus probably did not designate himself 'Son of God' in so many words, the real root of the post-Easter title lies in the relationship to God as Father."
6. Werner Kramer, *Christ, Lord, Son of God* (London: SCM Press, 1966), pp. 11ff.
7. E. Vogelsang, *Der angefochtene Christus bei Luther* (Berlin: De Gruyter, 1932); Jürgen Moltmann, *The Crucified God* (San Francisco: Harper & Row, 1974).
8. W. Popkes, *Christus Traditus: Eine Untersuchung zum Begriff der Dahingabe im Neuen Testament* (Zurich: Zwingli Verlag, 1967).
9. Jürgen Moltmann, *Theology of Hope* (San Francisco: Harper & Row, 1967), pp. 172ff.
10. W. Thusing, *Erhohungsvorstellung und Parusieerwartung in der altesten nachosterlichen Christologie* (Stuttgart: Verlag Katholisches Bibelwerk, 1969).
11. Jürgen Moltmann, "The Motherly Father: Is Trinitarian Patripassianism Replacing Theological Patriarchalism?" *Concilium* 17, no. 3 (1981): 51-56.

6. The Social Understanding of the Trinity

1. Calvin, *Institutes of the Christian Religion* 1.1.1; Cf. Martin Luther, "First Commandment" in the *Large Catechism*; also compare Gerhard Ebeling, "Cognitio Dei et Hominis," *Lutherstudien* 1(1971): 221ff. The fundamental cleavage between knowledge of the self and knowledge of the external world frequently encountered since Kant has led to a "theology of the transcendental subjectivity of human beings." For a critical treatment of this view, see Jürgen Moltmann, *Theology of Hope* (San Francisco: Harper & Row, 1967).

2. Erich Peterson, "Monotheismus als politisches Problem," in *Theologische Traktate* (Munich: Kosel-Verlag, 1951), pp. 45-148; for a critical treatment, see *Monotheismus als politisches Problem?* ed. Al Schindler (Gütersloh: Gütersloher Verlagshaus Mohn, 1978).

3. Cf. also Thomas Aquinas, *Summa Theologica*, 1, q. 103, a. 3: "Optima autem gubernatio est quae fit per unum. Unitas autem pertinet ad rationem bonitatis. Unde multitudo melius gubernatur per unum quam per plures. Relinquitur ergo quod gubernatio mundi, quae est optima, sit ab uno gubernante. Et hoc est quod Philosophus dicit in XII *Metaphy.*: 'Entia nolunt disponi male, nec bonum pluralitas principatuum; unus ergo princeps.'"

4. "Praeceptum aeterni Dei: In coelo non est nisi unus Deus aeternus super terram non sit nisi unus Dominus Chingischan, filius Dei. Hoc est verbum quod vobis dictum est." Cited in M. de Ferdinandy, *Tschingis Khan* (Hamburg: Rowohlt, 1958), p. 153.

5. Erich Neumann, *Die grosse Mutter* (Olten, 1974); E. Bornemann, *Das Patriarchat* (Frankfurt: S. Fischer, 1975); Rosemary Radford Ruether, *New Woman—New Earth* (New York: Seabury Press, 1978).

6. Aristotle, *Metaphysics*, 1072, a. 30ff. How does the unmoved mover move the universe? "He moves as one being moved without any motion in himself."

7. Late medieval nominalism reduced the essence of God to omnipotent will, which eventually led to political despotism.

8. Michael Schmaus, *Die psychologische Trinitätslehre des hl. Augustinus* (Münster: Aschendorff, 1927), pp. 222ff.

9. This way of thinking still dominates Karl Rahner and Karl Barth. It became obligatory for Western theology.

10. For a detailed discussion of the following, see Jürgen Moltmann in *The Trinity and the Kingdom* (San Francisco: Harper & Row, 1981).

11. Augustine, *Sermo 71*, c. 15 (Mauriner edition, 5:458/9); *Quaest. de Trinitate et de Genesis I* (8.1173): "Opera sanctae Trinitatis ad intra sunt divisa, ad extra sunt indivisa."

12. Karl Barth, *Church Dogmatics*, 1/1 (New York: Charles Scribner's Sons, 1936); Karl Rahner, "Der Dreifaltige Gott als Transzendenter Urgrund der Heilsgeschichte," in *Mysterium Salutis*, ed. J. Feiner (Einsiedeln: Benziger, 1967), vol. 2.

13. Cf. Karl Barth, *Church Dogmatics*, 3/4, on the subordination of woman to man. See D.S. Bailey's criticism of this view in *The Man-Woman Relation in Christian Thought* (London, 1959) p. 298.

14. Cf. Karl Barth, *Church Dogmatics*, 3/2, on the subordination of the body to the soul. Barth's understanding of soul and body corresponds to his understanding of man and woman; his understanding of man and woman corresponds to his understanding of heaven and earth. This strange correlation has been traditional since Aristotle. Cf. Ruether, *New Woman—New Earth*.

132

15. For a detailed discussion of the following, see Moltmann, *The Trinity and the Kingdom*.

16. Gregory of Nazianzus, *Fünf theologische Reden*, ed. J. Barbel (Düsseldorf: Patmos-Verlag, 1963), p. 239.

17. Augustine, *De Trinitate* 12, c. 5; also Thomas Aquinas, *Summa Theologica*, Ia, q. 83, a. 4: "Sed quantum as aliquid secundarium imago Dei invenitur in viro sec. quod non invenitur in muliere, nam vir est principium muleris sicut Deus est principium et finis totius creaturae." See also K. E. Borresen, *Subordination et équivalence: Nature et rôle de la femme d'apres Augustin et Thomas d'Aquin* (Oslo and Paris, 1968).

18. Schmaus, *Psychologische Trinitätslehre*, p. 189.

19. G. Mar Osthathios, *Theology of a Classless Society* (London: Lutterworth Press, 1979), pp. 92ff., 147ff.

20 P. de Boer, *Fatherhood and Motherhood in Israelite and Judean Piety* (Leiden: Brill, 1974).

21. Gershom Scholem, *Von der Mystischen Gestalt der Gottheit* (Frankfurt: Suhrkamp, 1973), pp. 135ff.

22. Nikolaus Graf Zinzendorf, "Die erste Rede in Pennsylvanien," *Hauptschriften* 2 (1963): 33ff.

23. R. Murray, *Symbols of Church and Kingdom: A Study in Early Syriac Tradition* (Cambridge, 1975), pp. 142ff. 372ff.; H. Dörries, *Die Theologie des Makarios/Symeon* (Göttingen: Vandenhoeck & Ruprecht, 1978); see also Elaine Pagels, "God the Father, God the Mother," in her *The Gnostic Gospels* (New York: Vintage, 1981), pp. 57ff.

24. P. Evdokimov, *Christus im Russischen Denken* (Trier: Paulinus-Verlag, 1977), pp. 134ff.; A.M. Allchin, *The Kingdom of Love and Knowledge* (London: Darton, Longman & Todd, 1979), pp. 167ff.; H. Koch, *Grundtvig: Leben und Werk* (Cologne, 1951).

PUBLISHER'S NOTE

Books mentioned in the notes are published in British editions as follows:

D. Sherwin Bailey, *The Man-Woman Relation in Christian Thought*, Longmans 1959

Karl Barth, *Church Dogmatics*, T. & T. Clark 1936ff.

Rudolf Bultmann, *The Gospel of John*, Blackwell 1971

Martin Hengel, *The Son of God*, SCM Press 1976

Edgar Hennecke and Wilhelm Schneemelcher, *New Testament Apocrypha*, Lutterworth Press 1965

Joachim Jeremias, *New Testament Theology*, SCM Press 1971

Jürgen Moltmann, *The Church in the Power of the Spirit*, SCM Press 1977

— , *The Crucified God*, SCM Press 1974

— , *Theology of Hope*, SCM Press 1967

— , *The Trinity and the Kingdom of God*, SCM Press 1981

Elisabeth Moltmann-Wendel, *The Women around Jesus*, SCM Press 1982

Elaine Pagels, *The Gnostic Gospels*, Weidenfeld and Nicolson 1981

Jon Sobrino, *Christology at the Crossroads*, SCM Press 1978